INTRODUCTION
TO
SIKHISM

125 Basic Questions and Answers on
Sikh Religion and History

GOBIND SINGH MANSUKHANI

SACHA SAUDA
GURMAT PARCHAR SOCIETY
2575 STEELES AVENUE EAST, UNIT No. 18,
BRAMPTON, ONT. L6P 5TI CANADA
TEL. : (905) 459-8351
FAX : (905) 459-5986

Hemkunt

© Hemkunt Press 1977
Twelfth Impression 2003

ISBN 81-7010-181-6

Published by :

Hemkunt Press

A-78, Naraina Industrial Area, Phase-I, New Delhi-110028
Tel.: 2579-2083, 2579-5079, 2579-0032 Fax: 91-11-2611-3705
E-mail: hemkunt@ndf.vsnl.net.in
Website: www.hemkuntpublishers.com

Some Hemkunt Books on Sikhism

For Children

Illustrated in four colours and black and white

The Story of Guru Nanak
Life Story of Guru Gobind Singh
Life Story of Guru Nanak
The Story of Maharaja Ranjit Singh
Stories from Sikh History I-VII
Sikh Studies I-IX

For Adults

Japji
Hymns from Guru Granth Sahib
Hymns from the Dasam Granth

(In above three books text in Gurmukhi and Roman scripts and meanings in English)

Introduction to Sikhism
Encyclopedia of Sikhism
Bhagat Bani in Guru Granth Sahib

Printed at India International Press, A-12/1, Naraina Industrial Area, Ph-I, New Delhi-28

FOREWORD

Eminent people of other faiths have paid tribute from time to time, to the noble ideals and principles of the Sikh religion and to our Gurus, but on the whole the world knows little about them. This is partly due to the fact that the number of Sikhs is comparatively small and also to the fact that it is not a proselytising religion and there has, therefore, been practically no missionary activity.

The world today needs to know about the Sikh religion and aboutGuru Nanak who preached the Gospel of universal brotherhood and love and about that great inspirer and leader of men, Guru Gobind Singh, who performed the miracle of creating out of a demoralised and defeated people the Khalsa, who became a symbol of courage combined with high character, of self-sacrifice and invincibility in the struggle against tryanny.

Great power, it is said, corrupts greatly. This is borne out by the facts of history, both in the case of nations and of individuals. Today we are on the threshold of an age in which man's knowledge of the forces of nature and to some extent, his control of them, has brought to man, power on a scale hitherto undreamt of. The great question of the day is; "Is this power to be used for good or for evil?" In the answer to this question lies the future of the human race.

There is a growing consciousness throughout the world that this power may result eventually in the destruction of all life on our planet unless man finds some kind of spiritual base. Guru Nanak's Gospel that there is one God who is the Father of us all and that we are all brothers irrespective of caste, colour or creed, is the most pertinent in a world of conflicting nationalities and faiths. Indeed it is the very basis of that democracy to which most of the world is wedded today. Service for our fellow human beings, fearlessness in the struggle against any form of social or political tyranny and a willingness to sacrifice all in that struggle, are the part of the Sikh traditions which is completely with the democratic ideal. When there are added to all this, the great character virtues of truth, sincerity, faith in the invincibility of man when he is fighting for truth and justice, you get the complete Man that the philosophy of Guru Nanak and Guru Gobind Singh visualised—Man in God's image.

Dr. Mansukhani's book is to be welcomed as a good contribution in this field. It makes available in language, easily understood by the ordinary layman, the basic principles of the Sikh Religion and the outstanding facts about the lives of our Gurus and their teachings. He has modestly called it an Introduction, but it is more than that. It contains much valuable information which should help to educate and enlighten people about a great faith and the Gurus who propagated it.

HARDIT SINGH MALIK I.C.S.
4th July 1977   *Ex Ambassador to France*

PREFACE

This book has been well received by the reading public, ever since its first edition issued in 1977. During the last few years, I travelled to different countries where many other questions were asked by those interested in Sikhism. I have therefore enlarged this edition with the addition of ten more questions and answers, thus raising the total number to one hundred and twenty five. In fact a new section has been added and some questions have been revised and given new numbers. Minor additions have been made in some answers. I feel confident that the reading public will find this edition more compact and comprehensive than the last one issued in 1982. A select bibliography has been added at the end. Suggestions for the improvement of the book are welcome.

October 1985   GOBIND SINGH MANSUKHANI

CONTENTS

Section I.   General

Section II.   God and His Universe

Section III.   Principles

Section IV. Sikh History

Section V.   Sacred Literature

Section VI.   Worship, Ceremonies and the Future

Section VII. Sikhism and Modern Problems

I. General

1. What is religion?

From times immemorial, man has felt the need of some power or deity to liberate him from his toils and to protect him from dangers. Further, he seeks to obtain peace and hope through contact with a superior power which is called Divinity.

Society and religion go together. Religion has occupied an important place in the history of civilization and philosophy. It gives a meaning and purpose to human life and satisfies man's longing for peace and salvation. Some form of religion existed in primitive societies. They believed in spirits, magic and images of gods and offered sacrifices to them. The basic forms of religious expression are sacrifice, prayer and ritual.

Religion has been defined as "the relationship between man and the super-human power he believes in and depends upon". According to Jakob Burckhardt, "Religions are the expression of the eternal and indestructible metaphysical cravings of human nature." It includes a rule of conduct or principle of individual life on which one's peace of mind depends. Religions offer different paths to salvation. The goal of religion is getting in tune with the Infinite. Moreover, the philosophy of religion satisfies man's desire for inner happiness and life after death. The impulse towards religion is an integral part of human nature. True religion is neither ceremony nor ritual nor going to the temple, but an inner experience which finds God everywhere.

Religion consists of a number of beliefs relating to a reality which cannot be demonstrated by proof, but which is an inexorable certainty to the believer. This reality induces him to adopt certain modes of action and behaviour. When Guru Arjan was asked as to which is the best religion in the world, he answered: "The best religion in the world is the one which stresses the power of prayer and the performance of noble deeds". Holy living or altruistic action is the practical side of religion.

2. What is the science of religion?

Some people think that religion is contrary to science because religion insists on faith, while science stresses reasoning and proof. But there is something like the science of religion. It includes two things: a general history of religions and the developments of a particular faith. While the science of comparative religion seeks to assess the varieties of religious experiences and a systematic analysis of their development, the history of a particular religion reveals the special features and deeper issues of an individual faith. It studies in depth the change in the forms and expression of a particular religion, the psychological development of particular communities in the matter of dogma and ritual. Connected with the science of religion are the sociological studies of the influence of social forms on the development of religion and psychology of religion which determine the place of religion in human life.

Theology must be distinguished from the science of religion. While the first is the pursuit of knowledge in the interests of a creed, the latter is a factual study of religious experience. Theology is based on the church, on the dogma. The religious scientist is objective and dispassionate. Religious science in its broadest sense is a history of ideas and therefore, has to find general answers to the common problems of life. One of the important ideas is holiness: what is holy as opposed to profane? Holiness creates reverential awe: The fear of God. An understanding of the basic concepts of religion has to be linked up with the practical demands of active and purposeful living. Metaphysics and the supernatural are beyond the realm of evidence. Their appreciation will largely depend on the widening of the frontiers of human knowledge and experience.

The inter-relationship between science and religion has been summed up by Prof. A. Toynbee as under:

"Science must be based on religion and religion must include scientific rationality. I think that the words of Albert Einstein. 'Science without religion is lame and religion without science is blind', are of even greater importance now than when he uttered them".

3. What is the place of religion in the modern age?

Throughout the ages man has believed in some sort of religion. It is thought that without religion he cannot comprehend the real purpose of his existence. In fact, religion has had a definite place in society and will continue to play a vital part in this age of science.

While science and technology might assist man in improving his physical conditions, surroundings and economic standards, religion and ethics help to develop his personality and inner self. Man may live in comfort and prosperity and yet have no peace of mind. Even in a highly affluent society like that of the United States of America, it is realised that wealth and power are not everything. Spiritual progress is intrinsic and shows itself in inner satisfaction and sense of fulfilment.

Moreover, modern society dominated by technology cannot be regarded as an ideal society. It suffers from great strains and a sense of frustration and futility. Science has now given the power to destroy his own civilization and the human race. It is religion alone that can save society from such a catastrophe and check the erosion of human values. It reinforces basic ethical values and discourages racial prejudice, economic exploitation and social injustice.

Religion like science is devoted to the service of man. Religion corrects the lopsidedness of science, because without moral and spiritual foundations, science can bring ruination to mankind. Religion and ethics humanise the scientist and make him realise his social responsibility. It shifts the emphasis in science and industry from exploitation and power to social uplift, peace and co-operation. Man must be the master and not the slave of machines.

Great scientists themselves realise the limitations of science. They look to religion to remedy the social evils. According to Dr. Julian Huxley: "Religion of some sort is probably a necessity." One need not accept the dogmas of religion, but one must appreciate its search for Truth and its endeavour for the uplift of the masses. Prof. A.N. Whitehead says in this connection. "The future of civilization depends on the degree to which we can balance the forces of Science and Religion.

4. Can I be happy without religion?

Much depends on one's idea of happiness. True happiness is a state of mind in which man finds tranquility and contentment. The external happiness conferred by material possessions and worldly activities is ephemeral and superficial. In Communist countries people may appear to be satisfied and contented as their material conditions improve, but can they really be said to have achieved true happiness and real peace of mind?

Perhaps one of the reasons for the present-day decline in morals is the neglect of religion. Without high ethical standards, which are the foundations of all religions no organised and disciplined life is possible. Promiscuity and sexual aberrations are no doubt due to ignorance and a neglect of the fundamental principles of ethics. In a secular state, it is the duty of parents and voluntary organisations to impart to children a knowledge of moral and spiritual values and ennoble them. If a man who is under a strong temptation thinks that moral rules are man-made, he may easily violate them. He will hesitate more to disobey them, if he believes that they are Godmade and have been revealed to him through a Divine Teacher or the Guru.

Even men of piety and great devotion are apt to fall a prey to temptation. There are such notable examples as Bhai Gurdas and Bhai Joga Singh. If religion is not sincerely practised, it has little effect on our private lives or that of the community. An interest in religion makes people seek the company of holy men, which can give them the solace and happiness they really need.

Some people make a show of being religious. This does not serve any useful purpose. What is needed is a positive attitude, to seek the company and assistance of those persons who are truly devoted to religion.

Some people think that religion is an irrelevance, a matter of no consequence, and that they lose nothing if they exclude religion from their lives. They believe in the motto: 'Eat, drink, and be merry'. But does this give an edge or meaning to life? Life has a purpose. Religion makes a man conscious of his spiritual heritage and goal.

5. Is fear the basis of all religions?

In ancient times, it is true that the fear of the unknown, the anger of gods and goddesses and the concept of divine punishment compelled people to believe in some sort of religion. They began to worship the forces of nature. In the Middle Ages, the Christian Church set up the Inquisition to punish the wrongs against the church. As man's knowledge increased, this fear was replaced by a conviction that behind the universe was a Creator, who was just and merciful and not revengeful or mischievous.

Fear is not always a bad thing. Fear of the police and of imprisonment makes many people abide by the law. The fear of venereal diseases keeps

15

many persons away from sexual over-indulgence. The fear of sickness has turned men's minds to research and the discovery of remedies for many chronic diseases and violent epidemics.

According to the new science of psychiatry, fear of any kind—particularly in the case of children—undermines their personalities. Instead of telling people about penalties for moral wrong doing they should appeal to their higher sense and considerations of the social good. It is in the interest of religion itself to discourage such fear and to strengthen the individual's moral values and social conscience. The moral code ought to be a part of daily life and any breach should be regarded as an injury to society, and against the best interests of the community.

Sikhism does not encourage fear. It does not believe in a system of punishment or the inducement of rewards. In place of fear, it advocates personal courage. It believes optimistically in the ultimate victory of the moral order.

Sikhism preaches that we should neither cause fright to anyone or be afraid of anyone. This healthy spirit has been responsible for the Sikh's willingness to offer his life for his faith. True heroism, requires a lack of fear and a lack of hatred. The Sikh believes in the cause he serves, without any idea of reward or punishment.

In Sikhism, the awe of God turns into love. Just as a faithful wife is careful and cautious not to cause any annoyance to her huband but rather minister to his comforts. In the same way, the true devotee is prepared to offer his all to please God and to serve His Creation.

6. **What are the characteristics of the Sikh religion?**

Sikhism is a monotheistic faith. It recognises God as the only One. He who is not subject to time or space. He who is the Creator, Sustainer and Destroyer of the Universe.

Moreover in Sikhism, ethics and religion go together. The inculcation of moral qualities and the practice of virtue in everyday life is a vital step towards spiritual development. Qualities like honesty, compassion, generosity, patience, humility etc. can be built up only by effort and perseverence. The lives of the Gurus show how they lived their lives according to their code of ethics.

Sikhism does not believe in *Avtarvada*, that God takes a human form. It does not attach any value to gods and goddesses and other deities.

The Sikh religion rejects all rituals and routine practices like fasting and pilgrimage, omens and austerities. The goal of human life to merge with God is accomplished by following the teachings of the Guru, by meditation on the holy Name and performance of acts of service and charity.

Sikhism emphasises *Bhakti Marg* or the path of devotion. It does, however, recognise the limited value of *Gian Marg* (Path of Knowledge) and *Karam Marg* (Path of Action). It also lays stress on the need for earning God's Grace in order to reach the spiritual goal.

Sikhism is a modern, logical and practical religion. It believes that normal family-life (*Grasth*) is no barrier to salvation. That it is possible to live detached in the midst of worldly ills and temptations. A devotee must live in the world and yet keep his head above the usual tensions and turmoils. He must be a soldier, scholar and saint for God.

The Gurus believed that this life has a purpose and a goal. It offers an opportunity for self and God-realisation. Moreover man is responsible for his own actions. He cannot claim immunity from the results of his actions. He must therefore be very vigilant in what he does. Finally, the Sikh Scripture (*Sri Guru Granth Sahib*) is the perpetual Guru. This is the only religion which has given the Holy Book the status of a religious preceptor. There is no place for a living human Guru (*Dehdhari*) in Sikh religion.

7. What is the need and justification of the Sikh religion?

The advent of Guru Nanak in 1469 came at a time of socio-political necessity. India had fallen on evil days. There was no security of life and property.

Guru Nanak rang the alarm-bell and saved masses from fake religions. Religion then was either by form of ritual or hypocrisy. He released people from the rut of formalism and the parrot-like repetition of scriptures. Guru Nanak challenged the division of men into classes, castes and communities. For him, *all* men were equally worthy of respect.

Guru Nanak stressed the uniqueness of each individual and wanted him to progress through a process of self-discipline. The discipline was three-fold: physical, moral and spiritual. The physical discipline included acts of service and charity, while leading a householder's life; the moral discipline included righteous living and rising above selfish desires; the spiritual discipline included the belief in only the One Supreme Being, (the Timeless Almighty) and the exclusion of the Pantheon of gods and goddesses, in whom they had formerly believed.

The Gurus brought a course of discipline to their Sikhs that lasted for a period of nearly 230 years till the creation of the Khalsa SIKH, the ideal man of Tenth Guru.

Guru Nanak opposed political tyranny and subjugation. He raised his voice against Babar's invasion and the tyrannical deeds perpetrated by his army in India. However, the imprisonment of Guru Nanak and the wonderful way in which he conducted himself and peroformed the tasks assigned to him in the camp awakened the soul of the Mughal invader. The Guru emphasised the dignity of the individual and his right to oppose injustice and oppression. His main task, however, was to turn men's minds to God. Guru Nanak opposed mere ceremony and ritualism as dead wood. True religion is purposeful and extals conscientious living, and not the tread-mill of ritual.

Other than for Guru Nanak, the lamp of spiritualism would have been extinghuished in Asia.

8. What are the distinctive features of Sikhism?

Each prophet gives some light and message to the world. Guru Nanak, the Founder of Sikhism, and his nine successors made a distinct contribution to religion and religious thought. Sikhism may be distinguished from other religions from three stand-points: philosophy, community or institution and physical appearance.

From the philosophical stand-point, the contribution of Sikhism may be called *Nam Marg*. Guru Nanak emphasised the need for man's devotion to the Timeless Almighty. He illustrates the attributes of God in his *Mul-Mantra*. He asks man to dedicate himself, day and night to the remembrance of God and His Name.

The Guru also gave to his followers the form of a community with certain institutions such as Deg, Teg, and Fateh. By Deg is meant the system of Community kitchen (*Langar*) maintained by contributions of the Sikhs. Everyone is to donate one-tenth (*Daswand*) of his income. Teg, the sword or *Bhagwati* represents power, which was necessary to preserve freedom of religious worship and to end tyranny. For this reason, Guru Gobind Singh gave to God among other names, the name of *Sarabloh* (All steel). The Sikh believes in God's *fateh* or victory. His salutation is *Wah-guruji Ka Khalsa, Wahguruji Ki Fateh*: the victory is God's and the Khalsa is God's. The Sikh always believes in *Chardi Kala*, (progress and optimism) in the reform and improvement of society, as a continuous process.

Sikhism also believes in discipline. Guru Gobind Singh gave the Sikh a new appearance and administered to him the Baptism of the Sword. He infused in him a spirit of fearlessness and a belief in his own invincibility and told him to maintain the five symbols.[1] (*Kakars*) each beginning with the letter K.

Another tenet of Sikhism is humility (*Garibi*). The Gurus asked their followers to regard themselves servants of the *Sangat*[2]. The tenth Guru, after administering his new baptism to the five chosen ones, asked them on bent knees and with folded hands, to administer baptism (*Amrit*) to him. In the entire human history, there is no other case of a Guru kneeling before his followers.

9.   Is Sikhism suited to the conditions of modern society?

The principle of "the survival of the fittest", is applicable as much to religions as to communities or people. Those faiths which cannot meet the challenge of their time or the new conditions in society are likely to suffer eclipse.

Sikhism however is suited to the needs of modern life. It believes in the individual and his right to develop his personality to the maximum extent possible. According to Guru Nanak, every man has power or merit; he is a part of the divine. He is not a useless weakling, a mere product of the chain-reaction of *Karma*. The Sikh is essentially a man of action, with an overwhelming sense of self-reliance. He should invoke the Guru's Blessing at every step in his life and ask for His Divine Favour or Grace.

---

[1]Kesh, Kirpan, Katcha, Kanga, Kara; (Hair, Sword, Underwear, Comb, Bracelet.)

[2]Congregation.

Sikhism is both modern and rational. It does not foster blind faith. Guru Nanak exposed the futility of meaningless ritual and formalism. He questioned the superstitious practices of his time and he brought about a revolution in the thinking of his people.

Sikhism rejects all distinctions of caste and creed. It stands for the 'Fatherhood of God and the Brotherhood of man'. It believes in a casteless, egalitarian society which guarantees equal rights to women. At a time when woman was regarded inferior to man, Guru Nanak placed woman on a high pedestal: "Why call her inferior, who gives birth to kings?"

An important aspect of modern society is the belief in democracy. The welfare of man is best secured by his elected representatives. This principle is the guiding rule of the Khalsa, which entrusts all decisions to elected Five Sikhs.

Sikhism also believes in the concept of a socialistic pattern of society. Man's responsibility to society lies in taking his contribution to social welfare as a sacred duty. The gulf between the more fortunate and the less fortunate has to be bridged. The Guru instituted the Temple of Bread (*Langar*) to break the caste system. This is a good example of true democracy in daily life.

Sikhism is thus distinct from other religions and has something new to offer to man.

10. Is Sikhism a faith of hope and optimism?

Yes, the Gurus prescribed the sovereign remedy of "The Name" as the panacea for all mortal ills. While some religions condemn men as miserable sinners destined to damnation and the unending fire of hell, Sikhism believes that there is hope even for the worst man. Koda the cannibal, and Sajjan the thug, were reclaimed to good life by Guru Nanak with the gift of Nam.[1]

All is never lost. If man realises his mistakes and shifts the centre of his life from the lower self to the higher self, he can attain to the highest goal. But this change comes through an understanding of the Guru's word (bani) and God's Grace. In moments of crises, even the most pious and

---

[1]Nam—the Holy Spirit, see page 65 in this example read "for a knowledge of God".

virtuous of men may succumb to temptation. Undoubtedly, evil and sorrow test the mettle of man, but his true support through all his trials is his faith in God and prayers for His Grace.

Sikhism is a practical religion. It shows mankind how to live a worthy and useful life in the world. It teaches him how to face and overcome evil through selfless service, devotion to duty. Man can work his way to self-realisation. If he trusts in God, feels that he is with Him, and that He will guide him to his goal. When a Sikh has to face trial and torture when everything seems lost, he prays for Divine guidance from his scripture, *Guru Granth Sahib*, and bears all difficulties with faith and fortitude. *Gurbani*[1] affords him true solace and enables him to accept the Divine will (*Hukam*) patiently. He prays in a spirit of dedication and not with the expectation of reward. A true Sikh never despairs even in the most adverse circumstances. He feels that he is in the company of the Guru, this gives him strength and he can then face every crisis with courage and an unshakable faith in God and the Guru.

Sikhism is suited to the challenges of the modern age. Mr. Bunker, ex-ambassador of USA to India, and a Christian, once said: "The Cardinal principles of Sikhism are very much akin to my own religion. It is a religion for our time".

As pointed out by Dr. Arnold Toynbee, "In the coming religious debate, the Sikh religion and its scripture the *Adi Granth*, will have something of special value to say to the rest of the world".

11. How does a Sikh reconcile himself to the secular ideal?

Sikhism recommends an active life—the life of a house-holder—*Grihst*—life in society, (not in isolation) where every individual makes his contribution to the development of society. There is no place for asceticism in Sikhism. Every Sikh must work for his living, and not be a burden on society. Sikhism lays emphasis on the right type of living—*Dharam-di-Kirt* (the labour of *Dharma*).[2] Worldly duties may be performed side by side with the search of "The Truth". A Sikh must set an example to others;

---

[1]GURBANI—The Guru's Word or Holy Spirit.
[2]DHARMA—Righteousness. This refers to honest living and Dignity of labour.

he should become a better farmer, a better businessman and a better public servant. He is not to shun material gain or the comforts of life.

"Salvation is not incompatible with laughing,

Eating, playing and dressing well". (A.G.,[1] p. 522)

Sikhism lays emphasis on man's social obligations. Man is a part of society and has to work for its uplift. That is why social reform is a strong point in the Guru's teaching. The Gurus rejected the caste system, untouchability, taboos against women, good and bad omens and the worshipping of graves, idols and mausoleums. Sikhism believes in the equality of man which is practically demonstrated through the institution of *Langar*, (the Temple of Bread) where all dine together in single line or *Pangat*. Inter-caste marriages and mixing on equal terms with persons of diverse faiths and nationalities is the norm. As stated by Dr. Gokul Chand Narang: "The appearance of Guru Nanak was a great step towards arousing consciousness of a common nationality."

Sikhism lays stress on one's duties as a citizen rendering service to the community as a whole. The sword is meant for protecting not merely the citizen but also all victims of tyranny. Guru Tegh Bahadur's sacrifice for preserving Hinduism from Aurangzeb's fanatical crusade is yet another aspect of the right of freedom of religion, which is so necessary in a secular state. Secularism requires an equality of all religions, without special favour to the religion of the majority or any designated as State faith Religion.

Thus, a belief in Sikhism is not incompatible with the ideals of a secular democracy.

12. What is the contribution of Sikhism to the uplift of woman?

When Guru Nanak appeared on the Indian scene, the place assigned to woman was low and unenviable. The tyranny of caste had left its marks on Hindu women. They had resigned themselves to their miserable lot. A widow had to burn herself on her husband's funeral pyre to become a *Sati*.[2]

---

[1]A.G. means Adi Granth—the Sikh Scripture. The page number refers to the Punjabi edition of 1430 pages.

[2]SATI—The ancient Hindu custom rejected by the Gurus.

The position of Muslim women was also far from satisfactory. A Muslim could lawfully marry four women. Who were regarded chiefly as objects of sexual gratification. Women were kept within *Purdah* (veil) and their education and movements were restricted.

The Sikh Gurus gave women equal status. They gained social equality and religious freedom. The false notion that they were inherently evil and unclean was removed.

Sikhism conferred religious rights on women. Some Hindu scriptures had allowed an inferior position to women, and affirmed that they were unworthy of performing religious worship. A woman was regarded as temptation-incarnate. The lot of a widow was deplorable. The Gurus exposed the folly of such notions. They rehabilitated women in Indian society. Religious gatherings and *Kirtan* were thrown open to women; they could participate fully in religious ceremonies and receive the baptism (*Amrit*) on equal terms with men. Guru Amar Das deputed some women for missionary work. Guru Hargobind called woman 'the conscience of man'. In religious gatherings, men and women sang and preached, without any distinction.

Guru Amardas condemned the practice of female infanticide and *Sati*. He advocated widow remarriage. Guru Teg Bahadur blessed the women of Amritsar and said that by their devotion they had made themselves "acceptable to God". Sikh history furnishes names of many women who inspired men to heroic deeds. The "forty immortals" were put to shame by their womenfolk on their betrayal of the Tenth Guru, and thus goaded to action they welcomed martyrdom and earned pardon of the Guru. They were returned to the Guru faith by a woman. In the Indo-Pak conflict (1971), Sikh women on the border formed the second line of defence and gave valuable assistance to our fighting forces.

13. How has martyrdom helped Sikhism?

No nation, sect or community can survive and prosper unless it has a band of persons who are prepared to die, to uphold its faith, integrity, unity, its tradition and way of life. That is what the history of the world demonstrates clearly.

The essential condition for entry into the Sikh fold is self-surrender and devotion to the Guru and God. Readiness for the supreme sacrifice, or of offering one's head on the palm of one's hand to the Guru is an essential condition laid down by the Gurus for becoming a Khalsa Sikh. Seeking death, not for personal glory, winning reward or going to heaven, but for the purpose of protecting the weak and the oppressed is what made the Khalsa brave and invincible. This has become a traditional reputation of the Khalsa. Right from the times of the Gurus till the last Indo-pakistan conflict (1971), the Sikhs have demonstrated that death in the service of truth, justice and country, is part of their character and their glorious tradition. They do not seek martyrdom, they attain it. Dying is the privilege of heroes. It should, however, be for an approved or noble cause. Sikh history furnishes outstanding examples of Guru Arjan, Guru Tegh Bahadur, sons of Guru Gobind Singh and countless other Sikh men and women, who laid down their lives to uphold the cause of the religious freedom and the uproot of tyranny.

Undoubtedly, in a world of evil and sin, men of God must be prepared to suffer for the cause of righteousness and truth. According to Guru Gobind Singh, the true hero is one who fights to uphold "The Truth". He then does not run away from the battlefield.

Martyrs face the gallows with a smile. The greatest tortures hold no terror for them. They look at the executioner with equanimity because they believe in the justness of their cause. A true martyr regards himself as God's instrument. Sri Guru Tegh Bahadur's martyrodom was unique. He sacrificed himself not to save any of his own followers but to save Hindu Dharm. Sikh History is replete with the glorious deeds and the heroic sacrifices of the Sikhs who suffered for upholding decency, truth, justice and moral values.

14. Does Sikhism insist on faith?

When we repose our trust in someone it means that, we have faith in him. For instance, when we send a child to school, it is on account of our faith in the value of education. In the matter of love, one has to put faith in the beloved. So faith is not peculiar to religion; it is found in almost every activity of life.

Sikhism insists on this kind of basic faith. Just as you cannot learn to swim unless you get into water, in the same way you can never know spirituality unless you believe in God. Sikhism enjoins faith in the Fatherhood of God and brotherhood of man.

Sikhism emphasises the need of the Guru for spiritual training. Fortunately, The *Guru Granth Sahib* is with us for such guidance. Many seek the solution of their spiritual and temporal problems in the Granth and seek light from *Gurbani*. We thus repose our faith in the Guru, discover the great truths enshrined in his message as our wisdom, acting in the light of *Gurbani*, tells us.

Sikhism enjoins us to love God. We cannot love God if we love ourselves. Ego is at the root of all evil and our sufferings. If we concentrate our minds on God and sing His praises, we subordinate and even drive ego out of our minds we can then acquire those great qualities and virtues, which we associate with God.

Sikhism believes in universal goodness. The Sikh seeks the God's Grace, not only for himself but also for the whole world for he believes in the good of all mankind (*Sarbat da bhala*). This sense of fellowship makes him feel at home everywhere and to look on all as friends: "No one is my enemy or a stranger," Guru Nanak wrote. He thus acquires an optimistic outlook on life.

The need for a Faith is recognised even by the greatest scientists. Indeed, reason alone cannot fathom the mysteries of existence and the Universe. Guru Nanak says: "The intellect cannot grasp what is beyond the bounds of the intellect. Rise above the limited human awareness and you will know of God and His works." Atomic energy and nuclear power have further strengthened the scientists' belief in the unlimited powers of Nature and Providence.

Albert Einstein writes in this connection: "Man does not understand the vast veiled Universe into which he has been for the reason that he does not understand himself. He comprehends but little of his organic processes and even less of his unique capacity to perceive the world around him, to reason and to dream."

15. What is the role of reason in Sikhism?

Reason and Faith are complementary. They operate in different spheres, though each is sovereign in its own field. Reason has certain limits. Faith is necessary in certain basic things, as for example, the existence of God, or the need of the Guru's assistance. Reason operates in specified fields, as for example, when a man shall pray and what actions he may take. Religion does not exclude the operation of the intellect, though it certainly acts as a limiting factor.

Guru Nanak challenged the superstitious practices and rituals of his age. He questioned the value of offering food and water to one's dead ancestors or the idea that child-birth causes impurity, or that eatable things should be cooked within an encircled space, made sacred by plastering it with cow-dung. He employed the touchstone of reason to test their truth and proved them false. He appealed to men to accept reason as their guide in all such matters.

However, spiritual realisation is beyond the ken of reason. On the other hand, great scientists of the world have accepted the higher truths revealed by religion. Man is an imperfect creature and his faculties and powers are limited. Albert Einstein observes: "Strange is our situation here upon earth. Each of us comes for a short visit, not knowing why, yet sometimes seeming to divine a purpose". Man is unable to comprehend the ultimate reality unaided. He needs the assistance of a religious leader or Guru whose divine knowledge and wisdom can guide him to hisspiritual goal.

Science continues to make new discoveries and inventions which, sometimes reject the theories of previous scientists. Could man 30 years ago consider it feasible to orbit through space or land on the moon? What may be regarded as a miracle at one time may become a fact later.

The theory of *Karma* is based on reason—the logic of cause and effect. This means that in order to ensure a good and bright future, man should perform good actions. How can man expect good out of evil actions?

Perhaps it would be best to have a recourse to reason when insensibility or blind faith proves of no avail. But where reason is obviously not applicable, we must rely on faith. This is particularly true of spiritual matters.

16. What is the place of morality in Sikh religion?

It is argued that one can be moral without a belief in religion. There are many people in various parts of the world, generally in Communist countries, who may not believe in God and yet are good citizens, kind and useful members of society.

All the same it is generally recognised that religion is a great aid to morality. Man is subject to temptation. Though he is born with certain good potentialities, the temptation to evil is so strong that without some moral background and religious convictions, he may easily succumb to it. In such moments of difficulty, when he is likely to be overcome by evil, the Guru, or true spiritual leader will give him the guidance and courage to resist it.

Ethics and morality are the basis of Sikhism. Evolution of the spirit is not possible without righteous conduct and adherance to social morality. Guru Nanak emphasises this point:

"Greater than Truth is Truthful living." (A.G., p. 62)

The Sikh follows personal ethics like telling the truth, gentle speech, fair play, service, humility and tolerance. Morality cannot be an end in itself. It is an aid to the evolution of spiritual life. Sin is a definite obstacle on the path of Divinity.

Immorality is something of which one is ashamed or which one practises in secret. The morality of Sikhism is based on the Fatherhood of God and brotherhood of man. Service for God is the service of His Creation. Acts of love and charity—even self-sacrifice—are not spiritual deeds in the strict sense of the term, but they do help to prepare the ground for the elimination of egoism. They show a love for humanity and a love of God.

Sikhism believes that this is a just and moral world. Though some bad people may seem to thrive, sooner or later, they will have their punishment. God is a strict judge and He treats people according to their deserts. Guru Nanak says:

"According to their actions, some get near to God and some distant." (A.G., p. 8)

But like any good judge, God is charitable too and tempers mercy with justice.

17. What is the place of sword in Sikhism?

No faith can survive unless it can defend itself. Sikhism was born in a hostile atmosphere and had to face a lot of persecution. In addition to giving Sikhs lessons in the art of daily living, the Gurus gave sikhs power to uphold their beliefs. For this reason Guru Hargobind donned two swords: one of spiritual leadership and the other of temporal power. He was the first Guru to throw a challenge to the Mughal power and to wage a war against the cruel and corrupt administration. His disciplined soldiers were successful against the Mughal armies in three battles. Guru Hargobind popularised the cult of the sword for purposes of defence and justice.

In a similar situation, after the martyrdom of Guru Tegh Bahadur, Guru Gobind Singh took up arms against Emperor Aurangzeb. He justified the use of force as the only means of survival. He wrote in *Zafarnama:*

"When affairs are past other remedies,

It is justifiable to unsheath the sword."

Where goodness and sacrifice cannot avail, violence has to be met by violence. Undoubtedly, in certain circumstances there are exceptions to the practice of non-violence.

The carrying of the sword or *Kirpan* may perhaps be questioned in the atomic age. In the present world it continues to be a symbol of power, as it has been in the past. On ceremonial occasions, practically all armies in the world wear it. Its carrying reminds one of belief in one's own self and therefore it creates self-confidence. Even Gandhiji justified the use of violence for a high purpose. The Sikh sword is a symbol of self-respect, prestige and independence. Guru Gobind Singh hailed it as the Saviour and Protector of saints and the oppressed. Infact he even referred to God as 'sarbloh' (All steel).

The sword is one of the compulsory symbols of the *Khalsa*. The Khalsa is ever ready in his uniform to protect the weak and suffer for a just cause. Guru Gobind Singh demonstrated in a practical way that the sword can be reconciled with spirituality. Goodness without the means to sustain and activate it will fail to survive. Therefore, it is right to say that the sword holds a very important place in the history and philosophy of the Sikhs.

18. Should we teach our religion to our children?

Some people, purely for psychological reasons, would not like to acquaint their children with any religion. They think that the child must grow up and then form his own ideas and select his own religion. They would give no religious instruction or moral training. This is not the right attitude, for then children in their formative years are denied the vital direction they need or like wild plants, their growth will be arbitrary and undisciplined. As children, they must ask questions and if they are not satisfied or receive vague replies they feel that something is wanting. They thus grow up in a spiritual limbo. The idea that when they grow up they will select a suitable moral code or spiritual guide does not work. Neither they will have the time, desire or opportunity, to do any thinking or searching for themselves.

Undoubtedly, children have a right to the best their parents possess in all phases of life, including religion. If the parents are Sikhs, they must make the effort to bring the truths of Sikhism and the noble ideals of the Gurus to the notice of their children. In the Rahat Nama of Bhai Desa Singh, Guru Gobind Singh called upon the sikhs to bring up their children in the Sikh Faith and give them Sikh baptism. To deprive children of religious instruction is to deny them the assistance that the teachings of the Gurus can give them. This will also mean that the vacuum in the child's mind will remain unfilled and he will continue to live in a state of uncertainty and moral ignorance. It is better to provide him with some moral ideas rather than none.

Let us make a more positive approach to the problem. It is not enough to encourage the social instincts of children. This may help in a limited way to make them realise that social instincts should have preference over selfish ones but the temptations in life are so sudden and strong that mere sense of social responsibility will not avail. A strong moral foundation is necessary to withstand the onslaught of evil ideas or bad company.

It is meaningful and rewarding to tell children of the benefits of the moral support of the Gurus and the assistance they will receive if they follow the Sikh ethical code.

19. What is the role of religion in human life with special reference to Sikhism?

The goal of human life according to some is the attainment of perfection, and according to others, it is the acquisition of happiness. Pleasure-seeking and fleeting joys should not be mistaken for happiness. Religion is the key to real happiness because it produces harmony by an integrated development of human personality and control of impulses, desires and thoughts. There can be no rigid approach for a human being as the problems of each individual are peculiar. Religion has to be flexible to suit the need of individual development.

Religion is the realisation of a "Divine presence" within oneself while leading a normal life. If divinity, progress and truth are not realised in human existence then the very purpose of man's life is defeated. True religion implies a search for the Truth and flexibility, in the individual approach to spiritual matters. Myths, forms and systems have fossilised religion and destroyed 'The Truth' and vitality in it.

Guru Nanak felt that spiritual development should not be crushed by outward symbols and forms. To bind the soul to the wheels of a socio-relgious machinery is a type of spiritual slavery. Freedom of the soul is vital for its adjustments to the needs of life and the complexity of social organisation. Constant adaptation is necessary for the achievement of harmony, between the individual and the Supreme Being. Man's nature is extremely complex and it is suicidal to chain it to a rigid groove or pattern.

Guru Nanak discarded all the prevalent supersitions of traditional forms of worship and symbols. He pointed out the absurdity of idolatry, hypocrisy, caste exclusiveness and pilgrimage. He challenged the use of intoxicants and narcotics, and the practice of Sati and infanticide. At the same time, he advocated the maintenance of ethical values in daily life: justice, truth, honesty, humility, fearlessness and gratitude. These qualities make a man a true citizen of the world.

The universality of Guru Nanak's teachings makes an individual approach possible. Guru Amar Das says:

"God! Save by Your Grace this world which is in flames. Save it by whatever way it can be saved." (A.G., p. 853).

II. God and His Universe

20. Can we prove the existence of God?

The existence of God cannot be proved in a scientific way by means of observation, experiment or other verification. This type of proof is possible only in the field of physical phenomena.

There are two types of evidence—direct and indirect. Indirect proof is based on probabilities and circumstances. Cirminals may be convicted on the basis of circumstantial evidence. Only the existence of God can be accepted on this basis of circumstantial evidence coupled with the testimony of saints and prophets.

God cannot be known through the five senses. Just as there is the electro-magnetic wave which cannot be seen, heard, tasted or touched yet it carries sound through the ether, in the same way, God's existence is inferred, though it cannot be demonstrated. You may as well ask the scientist to show you electric energy or magnetism.

Moreover, the personal testimony of saints who have realised God is acceptable as is the large percentage of our knowledge which comes to us second-hand. There is little that we know through direct experience.

The existence of the universe and the design or pattern behind it make people feel that it could not "just have happened", that there is a Great Designer. Just as a big mansion cannot be built without a master-builder or architect, in the same way, the universe must have been created by a Master-Designer who we designate as God.

Our awareness of a moral sense within the individual is also a reflection of some moral order in the universe. We know that truth is better than a lie, love better than hate. Where did these beliefs come from? They are an indication of the Creator who requires respect for these values in life. The Sikh Gurus never felt the need to prove the existence of God. They regarded Him as everpresent, not in theory but in fact. Guru Nanak thought Him visible and manifest.

Modern scientists and thinkers have come to realise the existence of

"A Power" or "the moving hand", which designs and controls the phenomena of nature. The pattern of the universe and the regularity of the laws behind its working confirm the belief that there is a "Lord of the universe".

21. What do we know of God?

Guru Nanak describes the attributes of God in the prayer, *Japji*: "There is but one God. His name is True and Everlasting. He is the Creator, Fearless and without Enmity, the Timeless Form, Unborn and Self-existing."

Sikhism rejects the theory of incarnation. God does not take birth. He is self-existent and not subject to time; He is eternal; He can be realised through (His own grace or) the teachings of a spiritual guide or Guru, but such a guide must be perfect.

Sikhism believes in a personal God. The devotee is compared to a bride yearning for union with her husband and waiting on his pleasure to do his bidding.

The Gurus have called God by different names—*Ram, Rahim, Allah, Pritam, Yar, Mahakal*. There is no such thing as a God of the Hindus or a God of the Muslims. There is the "Only One God" who is a presence, and is called *Wahguru* by the Sikhs (wonderful enlightener and wonderful Lord).

Is God transcendental or immanent? He is both. He is present in all things and yet they do not cover His limitless expanse. When God is seen through the universe, we think of Him as *Sargun* (Quality-ful); when we realise His transcendence, we think of Him as *Nirgun* (Abstract). Truly speaking, God is both in and above the universe. God is the Whole and the world a part of that Whole.

A complete knowledge of God is impossible. Guru Nanak says, "Only one who is as great as He, can know Him fully." We can only have some glimpses of Him from His works. The universe is His sport in which He takes delight. The world is a play of the Infinite in the field of the finite.

By His order, all forms and creatures came into existence. It is the duty of man to study the laws of the universe and to realise the greatness and glory of the Supreme Being. He has created an infinite number of worlds and constellations. The world in which we live is a small atom as compared to other worlds. Scientists like James Jeans, Hoyle and Narlikar have confirmed this theory.

22. Can we exist without a belief in God?

There are atheists who deny the existence of God. They are in a way free from moral rules and the stings of conscience. However, the atheist finds no meaning and purpose of life. He misses the inspiration and consolation of religion. He misses the companionship of God and Guru, and has, no future to hope for.

Again, there are agnostics who are not certain about God, because they do not wish to get 'involved'. They fear that religion may entail austerity and sacrifice. Such people regard religion as a gamble and are not prepared to take the plunge.

In Sikhism, the belief in the existence of God is a must. The disciple knows that God is knowable, but is not known to him. It is for him to study the scriptures and follow the instructions of the Guru to learn about God. A thorough knowledge, serious effort and steadfast devotion are necessary.

Moreover having a belief in God turns men's minds to His qualities: love, justice, charity, mercy, peace, wisdom, truth, goodness and beauty. When we meditate on His qualities, we imbibe often unknowingly some of these traits. Throughout the ages, prophets have given their concepts of the Creator. To the Christians, God is revealed as a Trinity: God, His son Jesus and the Holy Ghost. The Hindus accept the theory of incarnation and affirm that God appears in human form to save the world at the times of crisis. Islam believes in the one God who gave his message to Mohammed the Prophet. The Sikh Gurus emphasise the unity of God. He is the Creater, Sustainer and Destroyer. He manifests himself as NAM, "The TRUTH" and "The WORD".

Undoubtedly, you can live without a belief in God. You can inflate your ego. But the spirit will remain stunted and starved. You can develop the spirit only through spirituality, which means pracitsing a devotion to God.

23. Can we reconcile the existence of a merciful God with the problem of pain in the world?

Undoubtedly, the world is full of evil and misery. Look at the many wars, slave-raids, tortures, concentration camps, atomic attacks. Do they not show that man, without a sound moral basis is worse than a wild beast?

The problems of pain and suffering seems to be rooted in creation itself. We find one species of animal or fish feeding on another. Think of the epidemics and plagues. Everything is subject to disease and decay. Earthquakes are due to a 'fault' in the earth's crust. These, in addition to the eruption of valcanoes, cause a great loss of human life and property. Some calamities like famines and floods can be prevented by human ingenuity. We do not blame God for them.

On the other hand, the world contains many lovely things: sunshine, flowers and fruits. The picnic-spots in the hills, the splendour of the sunrise and sunset show that this world is full of beauty, Farid said, "The world is a beautiful garden."

God's purpose in creating the universe is to watch His play, to see how men and women behave in different circumstances. He has given man reason and freedom. Man may do good or evil. All his acts are recorded and he gets rewarded or punished accordingly.

Sikhism believes in a just, and merciful God. God does not, on His own cause suffering: "The Creator takes no blame to Himself." All things work under His law, He does not undermine His own law by making exceptions. Man sows the seed of action and gets the fruit accordingly. God is like a supreme judge who deals with people according to their deserts. It is also His privilege to pardon an erring but repentant soul. A deep study of the problem of pain makes us feel that pain has a good and useful purpose to serve. It draws out great kindness and compassion in this hard world. Pain is also a test, an ordeal, to assess man's conviction and courage. According to Guru Nanak, "Pain is a remedy, and pleasure the disease." Physically, pain is an index of ill-health, a kind of alarm-bell. When you feel physical pain you consult the doctor. Why not also do so for spiritual pain? God gives us timely warning through our conscience. Our Guru is the Doctor for these pains.

24. What was God's purpose in creating man?

It may never be possible to understand fully God's purpose in creating man, but prophets have told us something about man's goal. It is generally accepted that God's purpose is for man to realise his divine inheritance while living in this mortal frame.

God made man in His own image. He put His divine spark in man which is called "The Soul." the soul enters bodily forms according to individual's actions. The wall of the ego separates the soul from God. This leads to the cycle of birth and death. Metempsychosis can only be ended through meditation or the acquisition of divine grace.

God is not a cruel monster out for sport with mortals. On the contrary, He is like a benevolent father. He gave man a good start in this life by providing him with all the needs for his upkeep at the time of birth. Just as the body is sustained by food and drink, in the same way the soul is nourished by virtue and devotion. When the soul progresses with the performance of good deeds and the remembrance of The Name, it becomes more worthy of a merger to Divinity.

Man is a focal point in the universe. He is the apex of creation—the final stage. Human life is the starting point for God-realisation. You cannot own salvation as an animal or stone. Only human life, offers this grand opportunity for spiritual attainment.

Man is made of spirit and matter: *Shiv* and *Shakti*. The spirit is subtle, while the body is gross. The body has to be cared for, because it houses the soul. A house-holder's life is the best life because it offers scope for acts of charity and social service. Escapism or ascetisism is not advocated by Sikh religion.

Life may be compared to a game of chess or cards. Where the individual does not frame the rules or control the game. The cards are given to him; it is upto him to play the game well or badly, wisely or foolishly. God watches over him and will reward him according to his efforts.

In the ultimate analysis, human life is a rich gift, not something to be frittered away in frivolity. If one fails here, one has to go through the cycle of birth and death. It is man's option (what he can) to save himself from this chain of transmigration.

25. Is the worship of God necessary?

God does not insist that we worship Him. In His generosity, He gives to all—the high and the low, the educated and the illiterate—even to those who are anti-God; Athiest.

Some people are under the impression that God, just like an army commander, demands respect and worship. God does not need man's flattery or praise. Guru Nanak says: "If all people start praising Him, it will not make the least difference to His greatness." Just as the sun does not need light of the lamps so in the same way, God does not need the praises of men.

God is not a Dictator. People worship Him from a sense of duty— *Dharma*. They are convinced that God who made this universe can be known and loved. Those who know His nature and qualities are wonderstruck by His greatness. In their ecstasy, they exclaim *"Wahguru"*, Wonderful Lord. They want to love Him as devotedly as a wife loves her husband.

Moreover, many people feel that human life is the supreme opportunity for spiritual attainment. A worldly man who makes no efforts towards spirituality stands in great danger of joining the cycles of birth and death.

A sense of spirituality is a sheet-anchor for the individual. It gives purpose and meaning to life. Guru Arjan writes in The Sukhmani Sahib, "The seed of the Lord's Divine knowledge is in every heart." Thus, a sense of emptiness may be replaced by a sense of richness. Only those who are egoistic and wallow in their material possessions, refuse to accept the comfort of divinity.

Man is not potentially evil, but is weak and ignorant. When temptation faces him, he is likely to succumb to it. At that moment, he needs a support, an inspiration. If he remembers his divine essence and calls on his moral courage, he will get the necesary strength to overcome the temptation.

A positive approach to God will yield results. Union with God is our goal. His great qualities—Truth, Goodness, Beauty, Love, Purity, Peace, Wisdom, Justice, Mercy etc. are the ladder to Him. By concentrating on these qualities, we through auto suggestion, imbibe such qualities. Man rises to God, while God stoops to lift man.

26. How was the world created, according to Sikhism?

God existed all alone in His abstract form—*Nirgun*—before He created the Universe. This may be called the state of precreation. God was in the state of *sunn samadhi*.* According to Guru Nanak, there was darkness and chaos for millions of years. There were mists and clouds. None existed except God. Guru Nanak says:

"There was darkenss for countless years.

There was neither earth nor sky; there was only His Will.

There was neither day nor night, neither sun nor moon.

He (God) was in deep meditation.

There was nothing except Himself." (A.G., p. 1035)

Then God willed the creation of the universe. he became manifest: *Sargun*. He diffused Himself in nature. Guru Nanak says: "Thou created all Thy Universe to please Thyself, to enjoy the spectacle, the reality, which is the light of Thy own Reality-self."

When was the world created? This is a mystery. Was this process of creation a sudden and impulsive one or was it one of evolution and growth? Only God who created it knows. Like a spider, God spun Himself into a web. A day will come when He will destroy that web once again become His sole self.

The *Parkriti* of three attributes—*Gunas* (*Rajas, Tamas, Satav*) was created by God. *Maya*, attachment and illusion are also His creation: Guru Gobind Singh writes:

"He created the Shakti of three Gunas;

The great *Maya* is His shadow."

Out of the five subtle essences—*Sabda* (Sound) *Sparas* (Touch), *Rupa* (Sight), *Rasa* (Taste) and *Gandha* (Smell) arise five gross elements: ether, air, fire, water and earth respectively.

The Universe is not an illusion—*Maya*. It is a reality—not final and permanent—but a reality on account of the presence of God in it.

This world is the abode of the Almighty and yet He transcends it.

---

*Sunn samadhi—state of pre-creation, state of contemplation of the void.

27. What is the microcosmic theory in Sikhism?

Sikhism accepts the theory that God dwells in the body. As such the body is called 'The Temple of God'. In one of his hymns, Peepa in (uru Granth Sahib Writes:

"Whatever is found in the Unvierse is found in the body, whoever searches it shall find it".

The microcosmic theory is here in a nutshell. The Universe is the *macrocosm*, while the body is the *microcosm*, that is, the body is a miniature of the Universe. The Universe consists of atoms, the body consists of atoms. Superficially the parallelism is true: the Unvierse is composed of five elements—ether, air, fire, water, earth—and the three *Gunas: Rajas, Tamas, Satav*, so also the human body has these elements. In the *Pran Sangli*, the comparison is further amplified. The sun and the moon are represented by human eyes; light and darkness are reflected in sleep and wakefulness; heaven and hell are represented by joy and sorrow.

According to Indian tradition, the *Tantrikas* dilate on the fact that the truth is to be realised through the body. The body is an epitome, a small index of the Universe. What we are, the world is. The physical processes of the Universe are paralleled by the biological process in the human body. Perhaps the understanding of the cosmos may best be done through the ramifications of human body. Guru Amardas puts it thus:

"Everything is in the body, the regions, the spheres and the nether worlds.

There are jewels in the body, there are stores of *Bhagti*.

There is the Universe of nine regions within the body.

Brahma, Vishnu and Shiva reside in the body."

In the body, which is an epitome of the Univcrse, resides the Lord of the Universe. The devotee explores the body and finds hidden treasures therein. Ultimately he finds God within his own self.

Physical sciences have not yet been able to unearth the mysteries of the Universe and the miracle of the human body. There are millions of solar systems, and our earth is a very small part of the Unvierse. Perhaps, the working of the laws of the Universe in the human system may be found in detail in the years to come.

28. What is the concept of Truth in Sikhism?

The concept of Truth—*Sach, Sat* is basic and fundamental in Sikhism. In the *Japji* Guru Nanak deals with the subject of Truth. The word "Truth" has different meanings in different contexts. The most important connotation of Truth is God. The Almighty is Truth (*Sat Kartar, Sat Nam, Ad Sach Jugad Sach, Hai Bhi Sach, Nanak Hosi Bhi Sach, Ap Sach Keenay Sabh Sach*). Another meaning of Truth is Virtue (*Apay Gun, Apay Gunkari*) which includes qualities like honesty, righteousness, justice, compassion, detachment, humility etc. The third meaning of Truth is; pure, holy, sacred. (*Sacha Chauka Surat Ki Kar*). The fourth meaning of Truth is that which is correct and proper (*Jo Kuchh Karay Sat Kar Man*). The fifth meaning of Truth is eternal happiness of bliss (*Tatah Tut Milay Sach Paya*).

But who can give the Truth? God being the source of Truth gives truth (revelation) direct to the holy and the enlightened (*Jis Tu Deh Tis Milay Sach, Ta Tini Sach Kamaiya*). Secondly the Satguru (or Guru) can give Truth to the devotee through his teaching and example (*Satguru Milay Sach Paya, Jini Wichau Ap Gavaiya*). Thirdly the *Sadh Sangat* or Holy Congregation can impart an understanding of Truth to the disciple (*Sadh Sangat Pavah Sach Dhana*). So God, Guru or Holy Congregation can grant the gift of Truth to a devotee.

The gift of Truth comes to the deserving. The Sikh must satisfy some requirements to be a candidate for gift of Truth. He must follow the Guru's teaching; he must do charitable and altruistic deeds; he must submit to the will of God; he must do spiritual cleansing through remembrance of the Holy Name (*Mun Davah Shabad Lagau har siu Rahau Chit Laai*); finally, he must pray for God's grace (*Jah Prasad tu Pavah Sach, Ray Mun Meray Tu Ta Siu Raach*).

In Sikhism greater than Truth is Truthful living. One must lead a life of Truth. He must speak the Truth, act the Truth and think the Truth (*Sach Karni Sach Taki Rahat*). A noble character implies the practice of humility, compassion, meditation and a desire to serve and guide others on the spiritual path. Such a devotee earns the gift of Truth and ultimately merges with the Eternal (God) like the rain drop losing itself in the ocean.

29. What happens to the individual after death?

Human life is just a stage in the upward march of the soul. The individual has got birth as a human being, after going through lower forms of life. Human life is the final stage in the soul's progress to divinity. It is for us to make the most of this opportunity and thereby end our cycle of transmigration.

Death means the destruction of the physical self. The ashes and bone-dust mix with the elements. But the soul which leaves the body, awaits a new dwelling. Just as a person casts off worn-out garments and puts on other that are new, so the subtle soul casts off the worn-out body and dwells in a new form. If there were no continuance of the soul after death, how could it become perfect to merit union with the Almighty?

Sikhism believes in the immortality of the soul. The devotee has no fear of the pangs of death. In fact he welcomes death, because it gives him a chance for the merger into Divinity. The evil person, however, dreads death. For him, it will lead to the unending cycle of birth and death. After death, man comes to the next birth according to what he deserves. If he has been wicked and evil, he takes birth in the lower species. If he has done good deeds, he takes birth in a good family. The cycle of birth and death keeps the soul away from Divinity. It can merge with God, only if the individual, by spiritual effort, has amassed the capital of the *Name** and thus lives with the Holy Spirit.

Guru Arjan in the *Sukhmani* dwells on the sad plight of the soul which is not endowed with the *Name*. The soul in its lonely march through darkness can only find sustenance in the word of God. Otherwise it feels the weariness and pain of isolation.

The soul—*Jiva*—is a part of God. It is deathless like Him. Before creation, it lived with God. After creation it takes bodily forms according to His Will. The soul is, however, nourished by virtue and meditation on "The name". The transmigration of the soul can come to an end by meditation and divine grace.

30. Is there a judgement?

Sikhism accepts the theory of *Karma*: That man is punished or

---

*The Name—The Holy spirit as understood by Christians.

rewarded according to his actions. Man's actions in this world will bear witness at the time of judgement. The messengers of the god of death—*Yama*—takes the individual to the god of justice—*Dharam Raj*—who is very strict like a moneylender. The scribes *Chitra* and *Gupta* who have written out the account are called forth to present the balance-sheet of his actions. What does the balance-sheet show? It contains a record of good and evil deeds.

The god of justice cannot be bribed or influenced. He is strict and impartial and exacts a clear account. Certain faiths affirm that their prophets will plead for their followers in the court of justice. Sikhism does not accept this idea. Man is responsible for his own actions and cannot escape punishment through the intervention of a spiritual leader.

Perhaps the Gurus borrowed the old Puranic machinery of *Dharam Raj* and *Chitra Gupta* to impress on the minds of people the need for righteous and noble action. Guru Nanak says: "According to one's action, one gets near to or distant from, God." Elsewhere, the Guru affirms that the judgement on man's actions determines the next birth or form for the individual's soul. The best action in the world is to meditate on 'The *Name*'. This alone can earn salvation or freedom from metempsychosis.

The law of *Karma* is inexorable. Man's life is a series of actions. According to Sikhism, "Conduct is the paper, mind the inkpot; the good and the bad—virtue and vice—are both recorded thereon." Man sows the wind and yet expects that no whirlwind will follow. Man's choice of action will determine his future and next life. However by repentence, prayer and love, man earns God's grace which neutralises his previous *Karma*. There is no accounting of *Karma*, for one who surrenders himself to God. The true Sikh in a spirit of dedication and resignation invokes His grace and mercy, thereby inducing God to exercise his prerogative of admitting an erstwhile erring but now repentent soul, to His kingdom.

31. Is there a hell or heaven?

Man is judged according to his actions. If he has done evil deeds, he goes into lower forms of life; if he has done noble deeds, he gets a human life again. The idea of hell and heaven is a mere hypothesis. The picture of hell as a place of varied and terrible tortures is symbolic:

"There is a stream of fire from which come poisonous flames.

There is none else there except the self.

The waves of the ocean of fire are aflame.

And the sinners are burning in them." (A.G., p. 1026)

Shaikh Farid tells us that hell is a burning lake resounding with terrible cries. It may be added that the result of a sinful life is its adverse effect on character from which ultimately comes suffering and torment. In short, to be in hell is to be out of the presence of God.

Similarly there is no actual place called heaven. Sikhism does not regard the winning of a place in heaven as a worthy object. The old Indian concept of heaven is of a beautiful place providing all sorts of comforts and luxuries. The devotee is neither afraid of hell nor anxious to go to heaven. In a way, hell and heaven are conditions of mind. The virtuous man is happy and contented, as if he is living in heaven.

The concept of hell and heaven is just a rough illustration for clarifying the doctrine of *Karma*. Hell and heaven refer to evil or good stages of life respectively and they can be lived here and now in our earthly existence. According to Guru Arjan, "Wherever the praises of God are sung, there verily is heaven." Likewise, the society of the wicked is a hell. The condition of an average man is described thus: "Like birds that flock in the evening on a tree, flutter with pleasure and pain, scan the skies morning and evening, wandering everywhere, driven by hunger. So the soul of man wanders and suffers on earth." The worldly man eats, enjoys and sleeps, unmindful of the higher things of life. He is free, and perhaps, may choose wrongly.

32. What is Hukam?

Hukam means order: that is God's order. By God's order all forms came into existence. The Divine Will is responsible for the creation, sustenance and dissolution of man and the Universe. Whatever happens is by His Will. *Hukam* takes the form of Natural Laws or Universal axioms. All the parts of the Universe are under His control.

According to Sikhism, true happiness is attained by accepting and submitting to the Divine Will. Guru Nanak says:

"How can I be truthful and break the wall of falsehood?

By submission to His Will, as it is ingrained in me."

(A.G., p. 1)

Living in harmony with the Divine will brings everlasting peace. Like a child, the disciple is to be guided by the elders. Everything emanates from Him and is, therefore significant. Saints and martyrs, in spite of occult powers, have submitted to torture and death in order to honour His Will. "Thy Will be done" is one of the basic principles of Sikhism. This does not imply the negation of individual volition. A Sikh must bring his will in line with the Will of God.

What is God's *Hukam*? The Gurus tell us that God's command is that one must merge one's own will in His Will. The service of God's creation is the best way of working in harmony with the Divine Will. Secondly, God desires that man who has the Divine essence in him should once again merge in Him and thereby end the cycle of *Karma* and transmigration.

Submission to God's Will produces a sense of humility and self-abnegation. When man surrenders himself completely to him, he regards himself as an instrument of His Will. He realises that whatever comes from Him is for his own good. Every misery that he faces is a sort of mercy. He is full of gratitude and prayer for all he has done. Guru Arjan says:

"What pleases Thee, O Lord, that is acceptable.

To Thy Will, I am a sacrifice." (A.G., p. 676)

The only antidote for egoism and vanity is complete surrender to His Will. Only by conquering the self, can one enter the realm of God's Grace.

III. Principles

33. What is the goal of human life?

Man's creation could not have been meaningless. It is difficult to affirm what God had in mind when He created man. But one thing is certain that human life offers a great opportunity for development.

There are three parts to man—the body, the mind, and the soul. The individual should develop all these three aspects. For bodily development, he must earn his livelihood and follow the laws of health. For the development of the mind, he must study and educate himself and cultivate his intellect, for interpreting the mysteries of life and nature. For the development of the soul, he should follow a course of strict moral discipline.

According to Sikhism, the individual soul has arrived to the human form after going through innumerable cycles of birth and death. Now at last it may try for the final spiritual evolution, so that it may be freed from further transmigration and return to its source.

The body must be sustained and maintained because it is 'the house of the soul' and so a temple of God. God and the individual soul are in essence one and the same. Man regards himself as a separate entity because of egoism. When the wall of egoism is broken man realises his identity with God.

God's destiny for man is for him to realise God's immortal aspirations through his mortal frame, by leading a pure life with and through his physical body, coupled with his own intellectual development. Unfortunately, man is totally obsessed with material things: clothes, food, ornaments, comforts and luxuries. He neglects the things of the spirit. He wastes his precious life in frivolity and makes no effort towards God-realisation.

Life is like a game of cards. The cards are given to the player; it is up to the player to play the game well or badly, wisely or foolishly. God is watching us. He is keenly interested in our efforts to do our best. Human life is neither a bondage nor prison but rather a vehicle to spiritual attainment.

The goal of human life is, to try, to integrate the individual personality, with God.

34. Is a Guru necessary for spiritual evolution?

Many religions of the world agree on the need for a spiritual guide. On meeting a True Guru, the ignorance of superstition is removed and divine knowledge obtained. The Guru sheds light through his message. What is important is not the person but 'The Word'.

According to the Sikh religion, liberation cannot be won without a Guru. The Guru gives instruction—through the use of a *mantra*—this is a means of invoking a union with God. *Wahguru* is the *mantra* for Sikhs. Just as a teacher is necessary for secular studies so for spiritual advancement one requires a Guru because he has realised God. Guru Nanak says: "The perfect Guru has dispelled the darkness of delusion from my heart."

The Guru Granth Sahib was installed as the permanent Guru of the Sikhs by Guru Gobind Singh in 1708, because the stage had arrived when the living Guru had fully discharged his office. The personal Guru now became the impersonal Guru of the Granth. The Granth presides over all Sikh congregations and represents the word of God in a permanent form.

The Sikhs, therefore, do not recognise any living person as Guru. The song-message of the Guru Granth Sahib is the Sikhs' Guru for all time.

The true Guru reveals the divinity of man to the individual. He shows him the way to cross the ocean of life and to reach the Kingdom of Bliss. Guru Nanak says:

"The Guru is an ocean full of pearls,

The saint swans pick up those ambrosial pearls." (A.G., p. 685).

Just as milk should not be kept in an unclean pot, so in the same way, the Guru will not pour his nectar (*Nam*) into an uncleaned mind. By practising goodness and the remembrance of The *Name*, an individual prepares his own mind for the Guru's message. After due cleansing, the Guru administers the remedy of the *Name* with suitable directions.

We are fortunate that we do not have to search for a Guru, because The Guru Granth Sahib is already in our midst. By following the directions of *Gurbani*, we can progress on the spiritual plane.

35. What are the traits of a True Guru?

In view of the need of a Guru, one must be on guard against a pseudo or fake Guru. Sikhism lays down certain qualifications and qualities for a Guru.

The Guru must be a perfect man who is able to inspire confidence in his disciples. He must come to their aid in every emergency. A Guru does not live in an ivory tower. He mixes freely with all sorts of people.

The Guru is not an incarnation of God. He is a humble prophet or messenger, invested with the duty of showing the true spiritual way to ordinary people. Guru Nanak says: "He in whom the Light is fully manifest is the Guru." He must be prepared to suffer for his principles. He must not claim any status or excellence for himself. He is fearless and without hate. He may come in conflict with hostile social forces, vested interests and evil people out to oppose him, but must deal with them gently and bear ill-will to no one. Guru Nanak compares a Guru to a ladder, and sometimes to a ship. All the Sikh Gurus had the same light—*Jot*—the Divine Spirit in them.

Perhaps one of the greatest traits of the Sikh Gurus was their humility. Guru Nanak regarded himself as the lowest of the lowly. Other Gurus also were meek in spirit. They accepted all suffering in a spirit of resignation. Guru Arjan and Guru Tegh Bahadur became martyrs to the cause they cherished and in spite of possessing supernatural powers, refused to exercise them, because the working of miracles is not in accordance with the Will of God.

The Guru occupies the highest status in the Sikh religion. Guru Nanak says:

"The divine spark is in all,

It pervades every heart.

By the grace of the Guru,

It may be revealed, then the devotee feels blessed."

Slowly and steadily, the Guru guides the development of the Sikh to perfection and if the Sikh be very lucky, the Guru transforms him into the Guru. The Guru remembers *"The Name,"* day and night and makes others do so. He is just like a boat, ferrying people across the tempestuous ocean of life.

Meeting a True Guru, is a sign of benediction. The disciple must prepare himself morally and spiritually for his guidance. He is a tower of strength, a beacon, lighting man's path in this dark world.

36. Did the Sikh Gurus perform miracles? If so, why?

Prophets and saints have performed miracles. A miracle is an extraordinary event which reason or science cannot explain. Science has not yet advanced so far as to explain everything. According to the scientists, miracles have nothing to do with holiness or piety. Miracles are "not happenings against the laws of God, but are the result of superior powers which God bestows on His servants." Men of God are able to do things which are beyond the understanding of the scientists' limited reason.

Sikhism accepts the possibility of supernatural powers, but like any worldly possession, they should not be used for selfish ends. A sikh should not run after occultism, because the greatest gift is Nam and not supernatural power.

According to Sikhism, occult powers come naturally through concentration on "The Name." Miracles should not be performed at the bidding of a king or a leader or to prove the greatness of one's religion or to confirm the faith of people in a spiritual guide. Guru Ramdas says: "The desire to perform miracles is a worldly attachment and is an obstacle in the way of 'The Name' residing in our hearts."

The Sikh Gurus did perform miracles off and on, but they did so out of compassion or to set an erring person right. Guru Nanak made the bitter soap-nuts sweet near Pilibhit, to save Mardana from death by starvation.

The Guru condemned miracles performed for personal glory. Baba Atal who performed a miracle had to give up his life as atonement for it. Guru Arjan and Guru Tegh Bahadur were requested to perform miracles so that their lives would be spared. They refused to do so and welcomed the penalty of death. The greatest miracle was not to perform a miracle, in spite of having the capacity to do so. As Emerson puts it: "Self-sacrifice is the real miracle out of which all the reported miracles flow."

Guru Nanak was asked by the Sikhs about his supernatural powers. He answered: "I can do nothing against the law of God. It is only He who can perform a miracle. The 'True Name' is the miracle of miracles. I know of no other miracle." Saintly people do not like to interfere with God's Will by performing miracles. The Sikh Gurus never performed miracles to convince others about their faith or to save themselves from calamities or penalties.

37. What is the relation between the Sikh and the Guru?

The word *Sikh* means a learner, a student. He is therefore to get his instruction from a teacher who is called a Guru. The personality of the Sikh Guru, is so influential that it completely transforms the disciple and shapes his life to diviner issues. This is achieved not by personal and physical instruction but by the belief that the Sikh incorporates the Guru. The Sikh "fills himself with 'The Guru' and then feels himself linked up to an inexhaustible source of power." e.g. by accepting the aid of Guru Gobind Singh, he feels terribly strong—equal to "one lakh and a quarter" in physical and mental prowess. He will fight all odds and lay down his life for a cause. He is the Guru's standard-bearer and will not lower or desert it. It is this kinship with the Guru which sustains him in a crisis. Bhai Joga Singh, when about to fail, was saved from such a moral disaster by Guru Gobind Singh.

The Sikhs filling themselves with Guru's own personality collectively becomes "The Guru" in the form of the Sikh *Panth*: "The Guru lives within his Sikhs and is pleased with whatever they like." The idea of religious fellowship, was given practical shape through *Sewa*, or service *Langar* or *Pangat*, where people dine together in the free kitchen, is another illustration of the composite character of the Guru in Sikhism. The idea of *Sangat* or holy fellowship—generally for the holding of congregational prayers in the form of *Kirtan* and *Katha*—led to the establishment of Gurdwaras and religious organisations. Collectively, the Sikhs are known as "The *Panth*"—the embodiment of the Guru. Guru Gobind Singh merged his personality in the body of the community when he created the Khalsa Army.

The Guru stands for "The Truth" and the practice of "The Truth". "The Truth" revealed in the *Guru Granth Sahib* is timeless and changeless. But the methods of implementing "The Truth" are left to the growing personality of the Panth. That is why the *Guru Panth* is never lagging and should be ever up-to-date to guide the Sikhs. All important questions today are decided by the community as a whole in the form of deliberated on resolutions—*Gurmattas*—which are given the Guru's approval.

Guru Gobind Singh totally identified himself with The Khalsa. He affirmed: "Through their favour, I am exalted, otherwise there are millions of ordinary men like me."

38. Can prayer change things or destiny?

Those who offer prayers sincerely, know the efficacy and value of prayer. Other people think that prayer may give consolation and peace to man but cannot affect physical events, because the universe is governed by law. If fire burns today, it will also burn tomorrow, in spite of prayer. Life is regular and smooth because of these unchanging laws. Though saints and mystics may possess great powers. What we regard as a miracle may really only be the "power of prayer" or the "working of a spiritual law." Sincere prayer is a supplication made to God generally without any personal motive. God knows of all the desires and sincerity of the individual. It is up to Him, to accept or reject a request made to Him.

Certain basic laws are interacted on by other laws. Aeroplanes fly, contrary to the laws of gravity, but in turn they are governed by the laws of aerodynamics.

Prayer may help in a psychological way, e.g. people who are made ill by fear or tension while the effect is physical the cause may be mental. In such a case prayer may also heal in the same way as medicine, but by removing the mental cause.

According to Sikhism, prayer can change man's mind. Just as dirt is washed away by soap, in the same way man's evil thoughts may be washed away by prayer and meditation. Sinners have turned into saints through the power of prayer. The example of Sajjan, the thug is well-known. Bhai Gurdas has cited the case of Queen Tara Lochan. Her lost sandals were restored to her by prayer.

Guru Arjan emphasises the role of prayer:

"The praising of His Name is the highest of all practices.

It has uplifted many a human soul.

It slakes the desire of the restless mind.

It imparts, an all-seeing vision." (A.G., p. 263).

Prayer is not mere auto-suggestion. At its best, it is concentrating on

God and His qualities. God is goodness, truth, patience, peace and love. When a man offers prayer, God enters-into his life and gives His qualities to the devotee. With such qualities and power, He can mould things. Others may regard such events as just coincidences but people who understand recognise them as the effect of prayer: "More things are wrought by prayer than this world ever dreams of."

39. Should we ask for worldly things in prayer?

Real prayer is deep and inward; it is a dialogue between man and God. It is being in companionship with the Almighty.

Man's friendship with God should enable him to grow like Him. In the fleeting moments of "vision", man forgets his body and the world he lives in. He unites with his Lord and Benefactor.

Real prayer is pure adoration and dedication. It has no ulterior aim, no worldly things to gain. Prayer based on material desire, defeats its own purpose.

Man has been described as God's bride. Just as the wife makes all her needs and demands to her husband, so in the same way, man makes his request to God. As a good husband would meet the requirements of his spouse, and give her guidance and help, so God helps his servants.

According to Sikh religion, worldly things can be demanded in prayer, but on principle, they should not be asked for. Things which render service to the soul and advance man on the sipritual plane can be requested. Guru Nanak requested God to give him contentment, humility and His Name. The remembrance and praise of God, is the only thing a devotee needs.

Should we ask for worldly things and He in His grace gives them to us, we never feel contented. No man feels that he has enough. He does not know what is good for him. When God does not grant his prayers, he blames God and curses His creation. God does like to bless him but it is sin or sloth which prevents the blessing coming through. It is Ego which prompts one to ask for this thing or that for oneself. This is contrary to the principle of submission to the Will of God.

Instead of asking for worldly things, the Sikh must put his trust in God and entreat Him to do what He thinks best. The Almightly never fails those who surrender themselves completely to Him.

In the Sikh supplication—the *Ardas* or general Prayer, a Sikh prays for the constant remembrance of the *Name* and the welfare of all mankind. The right prayer creates hope, confidence and courage in the individual.

40. What is the Sikh prayer?

A part of the prayer called the 'Ardas' was given to the Sikhs by Guru Gobind Singh. The first part invokes God and the blessings of first nine Gurus. The second part recounts the events in the life of the Tenth Guru, the subsequent Sikh history, the struggles faced and the sacrifices made, for the reform of temples and the maintenance of Sikh tradition. The third part pertains to the individual's own thoughts and any special purpose or the occasion for it. In the end, the Sikh prays for humble mind and sound intellect, the victory of the Khalsa *Panth*, "*the Word*" and betterment of the humanity.

A Sikh believes in a personal God to whom he must go every now and then because he regards Him as friend and benefactor. He recites a prayer before he starts any work or business. Even if he has no time for a full *Ardas*, he shall make a short prayer.

Sikh prayer can be led by any man or woman; it is congregational in the nature of its contents. It recounts the sacrifices of Sikhs but makes no mention of the enemies of the Sikhs. The basic idea is to inspire the Sikhs to similar heroic deed in any future times of need.

Prayer is a means of ridding the mind of its ills and desires and filling it with pure thoughts and noble aspirations. True prayer requires an effort of heart-searching, an effort to become more pure and noble. The mind must be emptied of all worldly thoughts so that peace may enter it.

The Sikh *Ardas* demands a complete surrender to Divine Will. Resignation to the Will of God will ultimately benefit the individual. Only then can God take up his problems and sort them out. The Lord will never fail him who throws himself on His Mercy. Moreover, this submission eliminates the ego—the wall which stands between man and his Creator.

The reading of the Guru Granth Sahib is itself a kind of prayer. We seek the Guru's command. He gives us wise counsel, but it is for us to obey. Merely worshipping the scripture without carrying its teaching into daily life is the very negation of prayer. True prayer is the practical living up to of the word of the Guru and a continuing effort, for spiritual development.

41. Is it possible to conquer death?

Death has been interpreted in different ways. According to the general concept, death is the extinction of the body and the sense-organs. According to Sikh Gurus, death is the forgetting of God. Guru Nanak says: "If I remember Him, I live; when I forget Him, I am dead". It is this forgetfulness of God which makes man enter the cycle of birth and death.

Sikhism was re-born under the shadow of the sword. Guru Gobind Singh, at the time of the creation of the Khalsa Panth, called for Sikhs who were prepared to lay down their lives. The acid test of the Khalsa is his readiness to give up his life. The Khalsa covets the best type of death— death in battle—while fighting for the poor, the needy or the oppressed or his Faith.

According to Sikhism, physical death is neither painful nor terrible. All must die because the physical frame is subject to decay. But there is something like an art of dying. There is a joy at the prospect of a coming death. Even the worst tortures cause no fear to the devotee. Look at the Sikh martyrs. It is no joke to be cut joint by joint, to have the skin peeled off, to be sawn alive, to be blown away at the cannon's mouth, or to be crushed under the wheels of a railway engine. Martyrs are the real conquerors of death.

Those who know the art of true living also know that of true dying. True living is dying to the self, the ego, and living up to God. True dying is the privilege of the brave who die for an approved cause. Aimless dying—for no cause—helps nobody.

To conquer death is to merit salvation. Death has a terror for ordinary mortals. They are afraid because they have not made any progress on the spiritual plane. They feel worried for their sins and fear of punishment for their misdeeds.

A 'True' devotee, welcomes death as friend and as a benefactor because he looks forward to a union with the Supreme Being. He knows that it is through the gate of physical death that he will be able to embrace his Beloved Lord. Death is nothing but a gateway to Divinity and Eternity.

This mortal coil may be shaken off an opportunity is there, to don the robe of God's bride.

42. What is Karma?

The scientific concept of cause and effect, action and reaction is called the law of *Karma* (in religious parlance). A man reaps what he sows. Is it not typical that in spite of the law of *Karma*, man expects nectar after sowing poison?

Just as our present life is the result of our past *Karma*, the present *Karma* will determine our future life. *Karma* operates in this life and succesive ones. The law of *Karma* does not cease to operate after death, because death is just a matter of physical disintegration, and has no effect on the soul, which survives.

God is the Creator of the first *Karma*, the origin of the universe, and the destroyer of *Karma*.

Good or evil actions by frequent repetition leave their impressions on character. A man doing wicked deeds. Continuously will turn into a bad character. This produces states of mind, like anxiety, fear and guilt, all of which will cause pain and suffering to the individual.

Karma does not mean that everything is pre-ordained and that man has no free-will. He carries his past *Karma* in the form of character. It is his own actions that make him what he is. Guru Nanak says, "The record of my deeds cannot be effaced because God has recorded them." Man has to sow seeds, the choice and the initiative to certain extent. He also has the ability to change the course of events even, though circumscribed by heredity and environment. God as the Ruler of the Universe controls the over-all destiny of individual. Like the prodigal son, sinners turn to Him only as the last resort.

Sikhism modified the theory of *Karma* in two directions. Firstly, efforts of the individual are necessary for improving his own condition. Man is responsible for his lot. He must not blame God for his destiny. He must think of the present and the future. Secondly, *Karma* can be changed by prayer and the Grace of God.

When an individual learns to submit to His will, he ceases to make new *Karma*. He offers all his actions to Him; he acts as the instrument of His

Will. According to Sikhism, all past *Karma* may then be erased through the association with saints, and meditation on "the *Name.*"

43. Is there Fate or Freewill, according to Sikhism?

Sikhism affirms the omnipotence of God and consequently modifies the concept of *Karma*. Man is not a helpless puppet. The course of fate may be compared to the flow of a river, while individual action may look like an eddy, or a whirlpool or a wave.

Man has a dual role: firstly, as a person in a particular cummunity and environment, working under certain limitations, and secondly, as an individual with a free will, wanting to do this thing or that to elevate himself. He is like a merchant trading with a certain capital. He may lose it or invest it wisely, to earn profit. He is free to sow the seed, but once he has done so, he has no option other than to reap the fruit. Predestination is responsible for the present; but the present gives us an opportunity to mould our future. It is just like the rotation and revolutions of the earth. The earth revolves round the sun and is influenced by it, but it also has its own motion.

According to Sikhism, man is an active being—*a Karma Yogi*—who has to overcome his difficulties with understanding and wisdom. The effort of the individual should take the form of detached action and not, feeding his ego. He must work altruistically—for mankind, and not for the self.

Spiritual effort has to be blessed by Divine favour in order to be successful. This effort requires self-surrender, to His Will. If man works selfishly—in *Maya*—he suffers; if he works selfessly according to the Will of God he is saved. This self-surrender is a conscious effort to win divine grace. The self-effort is to bring the Divine Will and individual free will into harmony. That is how the two wills become reconciled. Man's salvation lies in his own effort to drown his Ego in the Divine Will.

Guru Nanak explains the point through a metaphor:

"The mind is the paper on which are recorded in the sum of our deeds—good and bad—the impressions, of the habits of our cumulative past. Against this, and limitless are the virtues of our Lord, for He turneth dross into gold and the fires (passions) of the body extinguish.

44. What is Grace?

If the theory of *Karma* were carried to its logical extreme, no man would deserve redemption. In Sikhism, the doctrine of Karma is modified by the "Principle of Grace". Man's sincere efforts and noble deeds achieve precious little.—What is required, is a constant solicitation of His aid in effort of spiritual endeavour. Recitation of *Gurbani*, meditation, acts of love and charity are merely a means to win His Grace.

An humble devotee, like the true bride, surrenders everything to the pleasure of her lord. Surrender to God does not mean slavery but freedom and the extension of one's horizons. Exemplary conduct, good actions and sweet words are necessary, but without Grace, they produce no result. According to Guru Nanak, *Karma* can be undone only by His grace. Just as it is the privilege of the Head of the State to pardon a felon who has been duly convicted by a court of law, in the same way, it is God's prerogative alone to redeem evil-doers and enable them to enter His kingdom. It is His privilege to grant Grace to those whom He likes. According to J.C. Archer, the Sovereignty and Omnipotence of God is manifold in his dispensation of His Grace.

The doctrine of Grace, does not mean that there are certain chosen prophets and chosen people, God does not have any favourites nor does he make any arbitrary choice. A devotee only prepares himself for being the recipient of His favour. He must empty his mind of evil and fill it with "The *Name*". This alone creates an awareness of the presence of God within one's self.

The Grace of God may come to the scholar or the unlettered, the high or the low, the rich or the poor. It does not depend on birth, knowledge, wisdom or penance. Those who seek His Grace through service and humility understand the purpose of life. Fire lies dormant in wood; one has to kindle it by effort. To realise this Truth is to get in tune with the Infinite.

The Almighty is so Grace-abounding—*Kirpanidh*—that the receiver shouts to Him: "Enough, no more" His bounties know no limit or hindrance.

45. What is Bhagti?

According to Sikhism, *Bhagti* (also spelt *Bhakti*) is a way of life, a dynamic manifestation of faith, a kindling of the mind and awakening of the heart.

Bhagti is absolute devotion to God. Bhagti does not mean living in an ivory tower, isolated from one's fellowmen. It is neither asceticism nor renunciation. It is the leading of a dedicated life in the midst of the world. Rivalry among different Bhagti sects is the very negation of spirituality. Real Bhagti is service of God's creation, Benevolence and kindness to all types of men, without distinction. It is both humanism and humanitarianism.

Bhagti may take either an outward or an inner form. The Sikh Gurus rejected outer forms like devotional dancing. They emphasised inner devotion, through love. Bhagti, rightly interpreted, is giving oneself away. Even if one is poor, one can share one's love and sympathy with others. This gift of affection, this pouring out of the heart, this outflow of sympathy and understanding, is the true worship of God.

Bhagti enjoins self-analysis and self-control. Both the body and the mind have to be trained according to the Guru's word. Guru Nanak says; "The body is the field, the mind the ploughman, modesty the irrigating channel, contentment the leveller. Pulverise the crust of pride into true humility, sow the seed of love—the seed of Bhagti—and it will flourish." (A.G., p. 595)

The Sikh Gurus developed the concept of Bhagti in two ways. While the Hindu saints and mystics discussed the academic aspects of Bhagti, the Gurus practically demonstrated it through creative literature, through hymns of adoration to the Almighty. That concept of Bhagti which was directed to idols and living persons was then modified to cover only an all-embracing devotion to the Timeless and the Formless God. Dedication to *Nirgun* (God) is the highest form of Bhagti.

A *Bhagt* is a practical example of a man God, a sort of superman, who by leading a life of ethical discipline, faces the problems of life and lives nobly and worthily.

46. Who is a saint?

A saint need not follow any recognisable form. He will be known by his qualities. A saint unattached to the five deadly sins. He must be pure in thought, word and deed. He is unaffected by the three qualities, of darkness, activity and goodness—*Tamas, Rajas* and *Satav* respectively.

A saint should regard himself only as an humble servant of God. He voluntarily surrenders himself wholly to His Will. He accepts God as his only prop and support.

A saint is not chained by the fetters of rituals, social regulations or public opinion. He is dedicated to the mission of *Bhagti*, spreading "The *Name*" among the masses.

A saint sees God in everything and therefore loves all. He lives in the world and yet remains unattached to its objects. Guru Arjan has summed up the characteristics of a saint in these words:

"The saint realises the presence of God at all hours,
He regards the will of God as sweet,
His only support is 'The Name.'
He is humble to seek the dust of all...
He finds comfort in melodious *Kirtan*.
He regards friends and foes alike.
He knows none as well as he knows God." (A.G., p. 392)

A man of God should not keep himself aloof from his fellowmen. He mixes freely with them volunteering to serve them and satisfy their wants. For him, no one is high or low. His love radiates equally to all. A saint is in the image of God. Meeting with him illumines the mind and confirms the devotee in "the remembrance of The *Name*."

A man of God should follow both personal and social ethics. He is just, tolerant, patient, modest, generous and merciful. He leads an ideal life and is pure and clean. He sets an example for others to follow, not through pride but through humility. He loves to save a lost soul like a shepherd going in search of a strayed lamb. He proceeds slowly and steadily to redeem the wicked ones and bring them to righteous path.

47. What are the five virtues, according to Sikhism?

The Virtue, of having the ability to do good, is a great aid to the achievement of peace and happiness. Selfcontrol itself is a great vitrue, because the mind usually turns to brooding on evil. Control over the organs of action—*Karam Indries*—is really necessary. The mischief of the tongue and the eye must be assessed or controlled. Bhai Gurdas insisted on the cultivation of sweet speech, toleration and charity.

Truth occupies the first place in the virtues recommended by the Sikh Gurus. According to Guru Nanak, "Truth is the remedy for all ills, it washes away all sin." Truth includes righteousness, honesty, justice, impartiality and fair play. A 'Truthful living' is actually a life lived according to the pattern set by the Sikh Gurus.

Contentment is another virtue. A contented mind is free from ambition, envy, greed and jealousy. Without contentment, it is impossible to acquire peace of mind.

Patience is another quality which a Sikh ought to cultivate. Patience gives courage to put up bravely with all the slings and arrows of outraged a fortune. Forbearance, particularly when one is in a position to punish one's opponent, is a great asset.

Perfect faith in the Guru is the fourth virtue which the Sikh has to cultivate and develop. Faith implies considering the Guru's teaching as infallible and following it in daily life. The Guru often tests the devotee. A True Sikh will never lose faith or follow any one except his Guru. Those whose faith is diluted or deficient cannot serve the Guru truly or gain the goal of their heart's desire.

Another virtue is compassion—*Daya*. This implies considering another's difficulty or sorrow as one's own and helping to relieve it as far as is possible. Compassion also includes the overlooking of imperfections and mistakes of others, for to err is human. The Gurus admired those Sikhs who observed others' faults, but did not expose them to their disadvantage.

The Sikh regards the practice of virtue as a means to an end. His goal is the integration of the human personality with spiritual realisation.

48. What are the five main vices?

Each religion has its own set of vices which its followers are enjoined to avoid. In Christianity, there are the seven deadly sins. Sikhism, regards as sin any wilful disobedience of God's law or principles of natural morality. Sin is a definace of the Moral Law.

In order to avoid vice, we must be able to recognise vice itself than develop the will to overcome it. In Sikhism, there are five cardinal vices:

Kam (Lust), *Krodh* (Anger), *Lobh* (Greed), *Moh* (Worldly attachment) *Ahankar* (Pride). These are the great enemies of man and cause much suffering. While they reside in the human body, how can the *Name* of God find a place in it.

Lust is sinful and produces nothing but shame and misery. Sikhism allows the householder normal, marital sex but any other indulgence is forbidden. Both promiscuity and sex perversion are absolutely forbidden.

Anger is an excitement of the mind which leads to quarrels and violence. Anger is overcome by patience and forgiveness. God dwells in every human heart, so one should not hurt the God in another man.

Greed is the desire for wealth or the love of gain. Money rightly used and earned by honest labour, is permitted. What is objected to, is an excessive love of money—especially money obtained by fraud or other unfair means. Avarice can be overcome by contentment. All too often excessive wealth creates an ongoing desire for luxury and the admission to vice.

Attachment is the excessive love of a wife, children or material goods. Regard your near and dear ones as objects of trust and service. They cannot remain yours for long. Any earthly love can only ever be transient.

Pride is the worst of the five vices. It implies conceit, vanity, jealousy or arrogance. It is the Ego, thinking aloud. The remedy for pride is humility. Humility, forgiveness and compassion go together. The true Sikh regards himself as being the dust of the feet of other people.

With the Guru's grace, these five vices may be turned into the humble servants of a devotee. Instead of their controlling the individual, they may do him service at his bidding.

49. What is the place of evil, according to Sikhism?

Everything is created by God, even evil. But what we regard as evil has a special purpose to serve. Evil is neither Satan nor any demon. This Dark Age, *Kalyuga*, (the age of sin) is the period when evil is likely to thrive.

The purpose of evil is to test the character of man. According to Guru Nanak: "Suffering is the remedy and comfort the disease." Man is inherently liable to succumb to temptation. The greater his faith, the greater the evil that challenges it. Great men have faced evil and tyranny—whether in the form of a persecutor, a traitor or one's own kith and kin—in order to prove the triumph of the spirit over matter.

The company of the evil-minded is to be shunned at all costs. It is the gateway only to the continuing cycle of birth and death. It is compared to an evil which defiles whoever comes in contact with it. Guru Arjan in the *Sukhmani* warns us against associating with Godless people.

The mind of man is more prone to evil than to good. Man is slow to take to virtue but swift to succumb to vice. Nonetheless, it is necessary to purge the mind of evil thoughts by constant effort, before good can enter it. Evil actions arise from evil thinking, motivated by lust, anger, greed, attachment or pride. Other evil actions take the form of lying, drinking, gambling, begging and backbiting. Sikhism does not believe in the concept of original sin, that a man has to suffer for the sins of his forefathers.

Perhaps the strongest shield against evil is to join the society of the good and pious people. The company of holy men has a positive role to play in spiritual attainment. In their company, one is influenced by their words and deeds and therefore becomes ennobled and pious. Guru Nanak suggests a remedy against evil: "Make Truth the knife. Let it be sharpened on the whetstone of 'The Name.' Keep it protected in a sheath of virtue."

Egoism is the greatest evil, because it creates a wall between man and the Creator. This wall can be only removed by submission to His will and the seeking of Divine aid. In his daily prayer, the Sikh invokes God's grace to keep him away from evil thoughts, words and deeds.

50. What is the value of fasting?

Fasting is good for health but has no religious merit. Some sects of the Hindus hold very strong views on fasting. For them, fasting has some real value and has to be strictly followed.

Sikhism does not regard fasting as meritorious. God has given us the human body—the temple of the soul—which has to be nourished and cared for. Fasting as an austerity, as a ritual, as a mortification of the body by means of wilful hunger is forbidden in Sikhism. Guru Nanak says: "Penance, fasting, austerity and alms-giving are inferior to 'The Truth'; right action is superior to all."

There are sects which do not eat this or that. Some people will not eat cereals, but will take other types of food. Such people may be treated as hypocrites. They give up the use of certain types of food, not because they want to, but because they wish to impress others. It feeds their Ego and does not earn merit. According to Guru Nanak, true fasting is the renunciation of the fruit of one's actions.

Fasting for reasons of health is understandable when done on medical advice. Some people fast regularly on a particular day in the week, so resting their digestive organs. It may also serve as a means to save food, or a method of balancing the domestic budget.

Sikhism encourages temperance and moderation in matters of food. Neither starve nor over-eat: this is the golden mean. Men who want to engage in meditation should only eat simple and nourishing food. Healthy food but in small quantities—Alap'Ahar, just enough to keep body and soul together and to prevent sleep and sloth, this is recommended for the devotee. On the other hand, gluttony is not only socially bad, but also morally reprehensible.

The golden rule about fasting is: Fast only when you must, in the interest of your health.

51. What is the value of pilgrimage?

Hindu tradition emphasises the role of undertaking pilgrimages as an aid for one's spiritual development. Sikhism does not consider pilgrimage as an act of spiritual merit. Guru Nanak went to places of pilgrimage to reclaim the fallen people, who had turned ritualists. He told them of the need to visit that temple of God, deep in the inner being of themselves. According to him: "He performs a pilgrimage who controls the five vices."

People go to centres of pilgrimage for a variety of reasons: some for religious formality, some for show, some for fun and some for a holiday. Some people delight in visiting holy shrines, in the belief that their sins will be forgiven. But bathing or other rituals cannot wash away sin. Real dirt pertains to the mind; it is inward. The growth of desire or Maya, cannot be removed by physical action. Nevertheless, visits to historical places connected with activities of holy men have a marginal utility. They remind people of goodness and tradition. Who knows when one may find some truly holy persons at a religious centre.

The futility of wandering to the so-called sacred places is amply illustrated by the life of Guru Amardas. Before he became Guru, he went on pilgrimages twenty times, without benefit. He saw the light only when he finally met Guru Angad. The Gurus tried to remove the notion of the efficacy of pilgrimage. Guru Nanak says: "I would like to go to pilgrimage only if it pleased God." Elsewhere, he says: "My places of pilgrimage are to study 'The Word', and contemplating its divine knowledge within me."

Guru Gobind Singh was very emphatic about the futility of pilgrimage. According to him, without God's Name, such visits have not the slightest significance. Kabir sought God in the temple of his mind. He therefore, migrated from Benaras, a well-known sacred city, to Magahar—a traditionally cursed town.

Real pilgrimage is any visit to the Guru which gives enlightenment. Guru Nanak says:

"No pilgrim-spot is equal to the Guru...The Guru is the river in whose water (Name), the filth of sin and evil thoughts, are washed off." (A.G. 1329).

52. What is true education, according to Sikhism?

The aim of education is to develop and integrate the human personality. The present system is lopsided and needs modification. Guru Nanak based the uplift of man on the cultivation of character. It is character which helps us to make the right choice or to take the right step in a moral crisis. Temptations come so suddenly that man has to make quick decisions. Unless one has virtue and guts both acquired by steady practice over a number of years, one may easily fall prey to evil.

The function of education is to prepare man's intellectual, aesthetic and emotional background in such a way that the individual's development is harmonious. They should follow *Dharma*, in its broad aspect. This includes reverence for teachers and elders, a solicitude for the welfare of neighbours and fellow-citizens and a respect for all types of life: birds, animals, plants with the emphasis on duty rather than rights.

Guru Nanak taught us of three Hs in place of three Rs; The knowledge of the *Hand*, knowledge of the Head and knowldge of the *Heart*. The education of the *Hand* implies the dignity of labour, self-reliance and of service to humanity. The education of the Head implies an appreciation of the wonders of nature, an understanding of the mysteries of the universe and a search for "truth". The education of the Heart includes the awakening of the higher self and the seeking of true inspiration from within.

Guru Nanak explained the spiritual significance of some letters of the alphabet to the *Pandit* and the *Mullah*. *Alif* stands for *Allah*, *Sassa* stands for an awareness of God—the Creator of the universe. He laid emphasis on character-building, citizenship and service: "The essence of wisdom lies in the service of humanity." Guru Nanak trained his disciple Angad through a creative and purposeful discipline. Just as a student needs a teacher, so a disciple needs a Guru. Men find it difficult to resist evil and do good, if left on their own, but if they are assisted by a great personality who possesses dynamic power, than their progress will be steady and significant.

53. What is conscience?

Within each individual is a source of inner judgement, which tells them what is right and what is wrong. Our conscience, is popularly called the voice of God. Even people who follow no particular religion have moral sense. They know what ought to be done and what ought not to be done. Even atheists who have done a wrong thing express remorse because they have later felt dejected and unclean, possibly due to the weight of public opinion or perhaps the moral sense that was engrained in them during childhood.

Sikhs believe in the moral order of the universe and know that God is both just and generous. He resides in the individual. The God within guides the human being through an inner voice. This is generally termed as conscienec. Within the individual, there is a perpetual struggle between good and evil. The conscience denounces evil and supports the good. We feel happy when we follow its command and unhappy, if we disobey it.

The effects of conscience—*Vivek*—differs with each individual, it depends on their stage of spiritual evolution. It is necessary to educate the moral sense. This is best done by associating with Holy men and meditation on "The Word". The conscience may waver at times in its firmness and power to control over human actions. Whenever we are in doubt—we must heed the voice of the conscience. We should respect its advice and follow it. In persons whose conscience is constantly overridden, this evil blunts and suppresses it.

A basic doctrine of Sikhism is to obey the Will of God. Where can we find the Will of God? According to Guru Nanak, it is embedded in the core of the human conscience. To follow one's conscience is, therefore, to live up to the will of God.

54. What is Maya?

Sikhism does not accept the conventional meaning of *Maya*—as illusion. The world is not *Maya*; it is a creation of God and as such, an abode of the Truthful One, or rather a Temple of Divinity. According to Sikhism *Maya* epitomises the principle of duality. It is this duality which makes one forget the Lord and attracts man to wealth, beauty, power or scholarship.

The root of *Maya* is egoism, the assertion of the self. It is this which separates a man from his divine self. By such fetters, man binds himself to his family and to worldly possessions. Maya is a trap for the soul.

Maya may also take on a more subtle form as self-importance or self-complacency. It may form different patterns like intellectual pride, family attachment, pleasure-seeking and money-grabbing. It plays an important part in daily life.

The Guru by his grace gives the antidote for *Maya*. It is "The Name" of God, which works the spell. With it *Maya* is brought under control and so no longer haresses the disciple.

The residue of *Maya* accumulates through many births. It sticks to the individual like glue. It produces an inbuilt sense of isolation which causes man to forget his own divine essence. The individual's soul will realise, sooner or later, that a Supreme soul lives within. This becomes a spiritual awakening which will secure liberation from passion and desire. This liberation comes through self-control and the practice of virtuous living. It is the association with the Guru and the company of holy men that facilitates this realisation of man's divine origin.

The evil effects of 'Maya' take longer to eradicate. Along with self-effort, the Guru's Grace is necessary. Guru Nanak says: "The true Guru has revealed the One to me. I have destroyed duality and can now recognise Him, through the Guru's word." Between man and God is a wall of ignorance, once this is removed, man may realise his kinship with Divinity.

55. What is egoism (haumai)?

Man possesses a divine essence. He is not separate from God, but on account of his self-assertion, he thinks that he is. He builds round himself, wall of egoism—*haumai*—which makes him forget "God in himself" and in all things. This is called *Agyan* or ignorance. Guru Nanak says, "Ignorance has its roots in the image of the self." Some feel that *Maya* or the materialistic world, creates the sense of separateness or duality, but whether *Maya* or ego, the separation of the individual soul from the Universal Soul is the cause of much misery and subsequent transmigration. Man's concern to build up a separate identity is the root of his suffering.

According to Sikhism, man is responsible for his own actions. Human self will—the ego—encourages man to bad deeds.

The egoism takes the form of a pride and vanity. These result from learning, power or money. They lead to arrogance and a sense of superiority which make one disregard and ignore other men. This not only alienates them from their fellow-men, but also from God who views with disfavour, any person who stands like a Colossus, in complete oblivion of the Source of All Power. Egoistic actions are like chains draped round a person's neck.

The cure for egoism lies within. If a man, subjects his will to God's Will and regards himself only as an instrument of God, he rises above action and its chain of consequences. Self-assertion is the disease, self-surrender is the cure. Submission to His Will removes the barrier between man and God. Guru Ramdas says, "The bride and the bridegroom live together, with a partition of ego between them. Once this partition is removed, the bride enjoys her union with the Creator." (A.G. p., 1263). Only when men understand that all things are subject to God's Will—including himself will he be able to live and move in tune with God. If, by the assertion of self, they cut themselves off from this Reality, they wander in the wilderness. But it is possible like the Prodigal Son, to come back to the bosom of the Father.

56. What is the Name (Nam)?

The word 'Nam' is derived from the Sanskrit Naman which means the practice of remembrance. It is a word used to describe the spiritual manifestations of God i.e. His Holy spirit. So the remembrance of God—Nam Marg is the essence of Sikhism. The repetition of the Sikh mantra "Waheguru" is an invocation of this Holy Spirit. Life without "The Name" or "The Word," or nam Simran* is barren and meaningless. "The Name" alone brings true peace of mind. The obstacles to "The Name" are worldly thoughts, sleep and occult powers.

"The Name" is inside every individual. The Guru reveals it to the devotee. The devotee does his normal duties with hands and feet, but he keeps his conscious mind in tune with His Lord. Some men practise "The Name" with the regulation of breath; they utter 'Wah' with inhalation and 'Guru' with exhalation. But this reflects individual convenience.

"The Name" performs three functions—it is purgative for the removal of evil; it is illuminative, because it gives us knowledge of "The Truth", Beauty and Goodness; it is unitive since it may bring one in tune with God. The remembrance is three-fold: with words, with the mind and with action. The repetition of Gurbani helps the mind to concentrate on God. It is food for the soul.

The technique of "The Name" follows certain phases—first the repetition of "The Nam": Wahguru by mouth; secondly, the percolation of "The Name" into the mind, (mental remembrance); thirdly, the longing for God like a lover waiting for his beloved; fourthly the awareness of God every-where; then finally, the ultimate union with Him.

Sikhism recommends the following plan as the easiest way to practise "Nam marg". Get up early morning and meditate during the ambrosial hours of the dawn. Avoid idleness and the five great vices. Seek the company of holy men, this is a great help to meditation. Try to maintain strict moral conduct, this too, helps you to a spiritual plan. Even then Divine Grace is necessary for the practice in humility of Nam Simran.

"The Name", apart from meditative aspect also means the "All-pervading Spirit." The entire world depends on "The Name"—God's own Holy Spirit. Therefore, to meditate on 'Nam', is to practise the presence of

---

*The remembrance of "The Name", invoking the Holy Spirit.

God by keeping Him ever in one's mind as also by singing His praises or dwelling on His excellences. From this may come the feelings of wonder and bliss.

57. What is Sahaj Yoga?

"Yoga" means union, and therefore, the means of merger with Divinity. Guru Nanak's way is called—*Nam Yoga* or *Sahaj Yoga*. The word *Sahaj* means the natural or gradual process. Just as vegetables cooked over a slow fire retain their flavour, so in the same way, the *Sahaj* discipline of mind and body, will bring out the essential goodness of a human being. Sahaj Yoga differs radically from *Hath Yoga*.

Sahaj Yoga is peculiar to Sikhism. It is the best form of the three traditional Yogas—*Karam Yoga*, *Gian Yoga* and *Bhagti Yoga*. Here the three types merge to form an ideal one. Actions which are noble and righteous, along with meditation on "The *Name*" and the elimination of the Ego, pave the way to God-realisation. In the *Guru Granth Sahib* it is called the Fourth stage, *Chautha Pad* which means that it is beyond the three *Gunas of Rajas* (activity), *Tamas* (darkness) and *Satav* (peace), and the three states—Awakening, Dream and Dreamless sleep. It is a state of equipoise, called *Turiya*.

The maladies of the soul must be cured in this life, otherwise they are carried over to the next life. For this a dedicated life of self-discipline is essential;

"I have placed the five senses under the control of my conscience,

By making my five organs of perception and my five organs of action also obedient to it, I became a perfect yogi."

(A.G., p. 208)

Just as the lotus remains in water and is not made wet by it, so the devotee may remain undefiled by *Maya* or worldly things. *Sahaj* also creates contentment and desirelessness. Man is, in essence Divine. No sooner does he realise this than he wishes to merge into the Universal Source. The wall of egoism may only be destroyed with the Guru's guidance and God's grace.

The union of man with God is like the consummation of marriage or like the confluence of two streams—*Sangam*. Such a union is possible, while living in the midst of worldly things and performing daily duties.

58. What is contentment?

Contentment lies in feeling satisfied with what one has. Some people question the value of contentment, because they consider ambition as the ladder to progress. The more one has, the more one seems to want. There is no end to ambition and greed. According to Guru Nanak, greed burns like an unquenchable fire; the more it is fed, the stronger its flames rise. A greedy man is never satisfied, even when he gets all that he wants. Avarice leads to many vices like fraud, lying and gluttony. An Avaricious man blunts his conscience and even bleeds his nearest and dearest ones.

Contentment implies frugality. Our wants are many, and our real needs few. Things, we can do without, cannot be regarded as necessities. Peace of mind comes from the elimination of wanting.

Contentment implies that life is greater than its wealth or riches. Regard money as a trust, real joy comes from giving and not in receiving. Moreover, excessive wealth often leads to luxury and vice.

Contentment is felt when one compares his lot with those who are less fortunate. Adversity is not a punishment but rather an opportunity for development. Moreover in poverty, there are few temptations and fewer flatterers.

A contented man remains content in adverse circumstances, be it poverty, distress or sickness. These are accepted as normal events of life, while discontented man increases his own misery by comparing his lot with that of more fortunate people.

Contentment results from submission to the Divine Will which a true Sikh accepts with gratitude and joy. Guru Arjan says: "Without contentment, it is impossible to acquire peace of mind." Peace and happiness come naturally to a stable mind.

59. What is humility?

As God is the Father of all human beings, any slight or insult to anyone is to injure God in every soul. Guru Arjan says:

"Know that God dwells in all souls,

And so become as the dust of the feet of all."

The antidote for the poison of pride, is humility.

The five organs of the senses—eyes, mouth, ears, nose and hands—are located in the upper portion of the body and easily confused by sin. The feet, which are located in the lower part are seldom used in wickedness. In India the feet are respected and touched at the time of salutation.

The vain and the arrogant challenge their peers and leaders. They seldom realise that there are other people who are better or more able than they are. They lack feeling of brotherliness. It is the awareness of human fellowship, which should make one treat all, with decency and consideration.

The Sikh Gurus set many examples of meekness and humility. When the old Guru, Guru Amardas was kicked by Datu, he never showed resentment but humbly suggested that his hard bones must have caused hurt to Datu's feet, Similarly Sri Chand, Guru Nanak's son, asked Guru Ramdas in a humorous way why he had kept such a long and flowing beard. The Guru replied: "To wipe the dust off your holy feet." Sri Chand was much impressed by the Guru's humility. Humility requires the elimination of the ego. It is the ego which is the barrier to self-knowledge and salvation. Pride is eliminated by understanding Guru's word. Guru Arjan says:

"Consider yourself the humblest of the humble."

It is the humble who are great and are exalted in God's court. True humility leads to a surrender to God's Will and the ultimate merger of the individual soul into Divinity.

60. What is renunciation?

Renunciation of the world—*Tyaga*—is regarded by Hinduism as one of the ways to spiritual attainment. Many devotees leave their homes and go into the jungles to practise austerity. This approach is disregarded in Sikhism, because this way or renunciation is not practical in Kalyuga* age. The mind does not find peace in physical solitude; rather, it wanders away to the missing worldly possessions and interests. As Guru Nanak explained to the monks of the Himalayas, "How will the world be served, if the pious people retire to mountain fastenesses and lend no helping hand in any attempt to solve the problems of the day?".

*Kalyuga: This age of sin.

The Gurus recommended renunciation in the midst of life—*Grahast-mai-udas*. The renunciation of evil desire and not the cessation of work or retirement, is the true way. Guru Arjan says: "Renunciation of lust, anger and attachment is praiseworthy." The true Sikh is the real *Sanyasi*.* He lives desireless in the midst of worldly possessions and associations. He does his daily chores and yet keeps himself free from attachment to he world. He is neither depressed by worldly affliction nor elated by gain or attainment. Like the lotus flower, he is not affected by the level of worldly things.

True renunciation results in finding mental "detachment". Kabir says,

"Do your daily duties with hands and feet,
But concentrate on the Lord."   (A.G., p. 1376)

Just as a mother who is busy in her household work thinks of her child lying in a cradle, so a true devotee, apparently busy in his office may still be repeating the Name. Guru Gobind Singh explains the point in these words;

"O, my soul practise renunciation in this way,

Consider your house as a forest and yourself as an ascetic,

Let continence be your matted hair,
And communion with God your ablution."

True renunciation results from the practical application of the Sikh way of life—a life of meditation and service to mankind.

61. What is the role of service (Sewa) without thoughts of self in Sikhism?

The Gurus mentioned the performance of selfless service on the part of a disciple as the first step in Sikhism. By doing service of various kinds without payment or any expectation of reward, one acts as a *Sewak* or *Sewadar*. From this may spring humility and the consequent elimination of one's ego in this way, God's "Name" can best enter an humbled mind.

What are the requirements of a true *Sewak*? He should have an absolute faith in the Guru; he must surrender himself to follow the code of

---

*Sanyasi: an ascetic, a recluse.

self-discipline as laid down by the Gurus. Voluntary service can be of different kinds—with body, mind and money. First comes the physical service—Shoe-care at the temple, the cleaning of the premises, cooking and serving in the Free Kitchen. Apart from serving *Sangat* (Congregation) one is also expected to serve one's family members, relations and the community. One may help in cash or kind, to deserving persons and charitable organisations. Then comes service with the mind, such as is required for reflection on *Gurbani* and the remembrance of God's Name— All these forms of service are recommended by the Gurus.

They also warn us that service must be done gladly and without any motive for compensation. It has not to be done with a secret or hidden ideas to win approbation, honour or position. These defeat the main object of "service" which is to eliminate the ego. Unfortunately, most Sikhs do little *sewa*, but expect a big return for what they do such considerations are unbecoming for True disciples.

The Gurus have enumerated various benefits from doing selfless service. One may obtain inner happiness and real honour. As one learns to be humble and associates with holy persons, and progresses on the spiritual path, so one may come to worldly success. Sikhism, requires a *Sadhana*—an effort towards the spiritualising of the self.

All the Gurus performed various kinds of voluntary service, both inside and outside Sikh institutions. The Sikhs then followed in their footsteps; we have examples of the services of Bhai Manjh, Bhai Hindal and Bhai Kanhaiya, to name but a few. Even today, we find various kinds of service organisations run by the Sikhs in India, like orphanages, widows' homes, institutes for the destitute and the handicapped, like the Blind school.

The important question to ask oneself is: "What service can I do?" The answer depends on one's own abilities and inclination. One may serve in any field in which one is interested. Any service, is a step on the path of Sikhism, provide it is done in sincerity and without thoughts of the self.

62. What are the stages in spiritual development, according to Sikhism?

Spiritual attainment is directly allied to personal development. Much depends on the amount of effort—*Sadhana*—the devotee puts in. Meditation on "The Name," joining the company of the saints, performing good or noble deeds all help one to progress on a spiritual plane.

Guru Nanak has mentioned five stages of spiritual growth in the *Japji*. The first stage is in the region of duty—*Dharam Khand*—here, man does act and reaps the consequences. Those who carry out their duties sincerely and honestly, enter the second region—the region of knowledge—*Gian Khand*. Here a devotee may obtain a knowledge of God and the Universe. He learns of his own human limitations, the omnipotence of God and the vastness of His creation. He may then realise that there is some further purpose behind God's creation. He then enters the third stage—the region of effort—*Saram Khand*—here his mind and understanding are purified. He endeavours to act according to the instructions of the Guru. Such efforts may lead him to the next region—the region of grace—*Karam Khand*; here the selfless devotee may find divine grace and develop spiritual power. Finally, only with the God's grace he may enter the next stage—the region of truth—*Sach Khand*—where he may unite with God. Such is the progress of man from the worldly to the spiritual plane. Undoubtedly, being moral is a great help to spiritual progress.

In Sikhism, the grace of the Guru or of God is necessary to help a pilgrim on to the spiritual path. It may be possible for an ordinary person to walk steadily on his own, but if he is primed by another personality, possessing dynamic power, he can further gather momentum, to go forward. The care and tutelage of the Guru protects him from many untoward calamities and encourages him through the many crises in life.

Guru Nanak laid down a way of spiritual discipline in the penultimate verse of the *Japji*. The devotees should exercise control over their mind and body, strive sincerely to walk on the spiritual path, use their reason when confronted with problems, fear no one and ceaselessly repeat the Divine 'Name.' Such persons will radiate joy and peace to all people who come near them.

63. What is the mission of the Khalsa?

The Khalsa was the creation of the last living Sikh Master, Guru Gobind Singh. The ten Gurus had given more than 200 years of training to the Sikhs and wanted to demonstrate the type of Godman who would be perfect in all respects. He would be a model of Sikh principles. Guru Gobind Singh gave the Khalsa "*Amrit*"—the baptism of the sword. He knelt before the *Panj Piyaras* and begged for *Amrit!* He said that the Khalsa was his physical form and the embodiment of all that is best in the Sikh religion. He gave them the uniform of the five symbols and the five *Banis*. They were to be saint-soldiers, devoted to the service of mankind.

The baptism of the sword was meant to create fearlessness in the Sikhs. They were enjoined to carry the *Kirpan*, for purposes of the defence of others and for the uprooting of evil. This mission of the defence of the weak and the downtrodden gave an impetus to a spirit of service and sacrifice. The Khalsa Panth had to meet the need of the times—to protect the weak against the oppression of Moghul rulers. History shows how the Sikhs bore the brunt of Moghul tyranny and indignation. The two holocausts—*Chotta Ghallughara* of June 1746, when more than ten thousand Sikhs were butchered, and *Vada Ghallughara* of February 1762, when more than thirty thousand Sikhs were killed—clearly demonstrated that the Khalsa was always ready to meet the challenge of bigoted Muslim rulers. In the freedom struggle (1931—1947), the Khalsa Panth, gave a good account of itself. During the Chinese invasion of 1962 and Indo-Pak wars of September 1965 and December 1971, the Sikhs won many official awards for their heroism.

Some people suggest that the Khalsa was created only to meet the needs of the time. This is not correct. The Khalsa was intended to prepetuate the ideal of the godly warrior—the saint-soldier—which the Guru Nanak and Guru Gobind Singh had in mind. Here was a harmonious development of physical and spiritual personality within the *Grihst Ashram*[2]. Here the best characteristics of past and present were fused together to create a man for the future—A Khalsa—dedicated to the glory of God and the freedom and dignity of man. Undoubtedly, Khalsas will come to the forefront in meeting any future crisis in any part of the world.

64. Are the five symbols really necessary?

It has been found that the maintenance of a similarity of appearance is essential, not only for the sake of uniformity but also for sustaining the enthusiasm of an organisation. Such uniformity should be a living demon-

---

1. The baptismal water prepared by the Panj Piyaras.
2. Grihst Ashram: The state of a family man; the married life of a householder.

stration of the inspiration of the personality that created them. They symbolise the ideal and make it more real and meaningful to the followers.

The Sikh symbols were not intended to create a spirit of *exclusiveness or of "chosen people."* They were meant to serve as aids to the corporate life of the community. It may be possible for a man to devote himself to God without adopting any forms or symbols, but if he wants to join an organisation, he must keep up the disciplinary forms of the group. One may be a good soldier without military drill and uniform, but that does not minimise the need for such in a regular army, in the same way, the Sikhs of Guru Gobind Singh stick to his uniform and the symbols ordained by him and find them a great aid in Panthic organisation.

It has been recorded in history that whenever Guru Gobind Singh was pleased with anyone, he welcomed him to the fold of the Khalsa. Lachhman Bairagi became Banda Singh. It is said that more than eighty thousand Sikhs received "Baptism by the sword", within a few months of the creation of the Khalsa.

The symbols have kept the Sikhs united. They have also helped to maintain their ideals in great crises. Many Sikhs faced death but refused to shave off their hair—*kesh*—which is the most important of the five symbols. The maintenance of unshorn hair is in keeping with the idea of living according to the Will of God. The kesh symbolise the spiritual link with the Guru-power.

Along with the maintenance of five symbols, the leading of an exemplary life—*Rahat*—is essential. Abstinence from tobacco, *Halal** meat, wines, narcotics and adultery is part of the discipline of a Khalsa. The code of conduct is a difficult one. Guru Gobind Singh valued the form of the Khalsa, and stated that so long as Khalsa maintains the symbols, he will march to glory; when he shows indifference to them, his lustre will tarnish and fade away.

65. What is the significance of the five symbols?

When Guru Gobind Singh created the Khalsa Panth in 1699, he ordered them to maintain the five symbols—*Panj Kakar*. These symbols were not only necessary for the strength and uniformity of the organisa-

---

**Halal* meat is a ritual meat prepared by members of certain faiths; the animal's blood is drained off to produce white meat.

tion, but also for the value they each had in their own right. Let us examine the significance of each symbol.

Hair—*kesh*—was regarded as a symbol of saintliness and *Dharma* in ancient times. The Biblical story of Samson Agonistes shows that hair was his source of strength and vitality. Guru Nanak started the practice of keeping unshorn hair. His son Sri Chand, the founder of the Udasi sect, also ordered his followers to maintain long hair. The keeping of hair is regarded as an indication of living in harmony with the Will of God. The shaving of hair may be construed as interference in nature's way and considering oneself wiser than God. Keeping hair is the most important symbol. A Khalsa becomes apostate—*Patit*—if he shaves or trims his hair.

The comb—*Kanga*—is necessary for keeping the hair clean and tidy.

Underwear—*Kachh*—is regarded as a symbol of chastity. Moreover, it allows unembarrassed movement in times of action. It is also easy and comfortable to wear when at rest. It serves as a mark of readiness and agility.

Sword—*Kirpan*—is an emblem of courage and adventure. In order to have self-respect, the Khalsa should maintain the means to vindicate his honour. The sword is to be used for the defence of others and not for offence. From the possession of a sword comes the Khalsa Panth to be a brotherhood of arms.

The steel bracelet—*Kara*—is a symbol of restraint and gentility, it also reminds the Sikh that he is bonded to the Guru. When a Sikh looks at it, he will think twice before doing an evil deed. These symbols are kept to preserve corporate unity and to foster the sentiment of brotherhood. They assist a Khalsa look exactly like Guru Gobind Singh (formwise) and thus hopefully prompt him to behave like a Guru.

66. What is the Code of Discipline for the Khalsa?

At the first initiation of the Khalsa Brotherhood, Guru Gobind Singh gave the instructions to the Panj Piyaras during the ceremony of *Amrit*. These instructions may be summarised as under:

1. Believe in only the One Absolute God, the Ten Sikh Gurus and *Gur Granth Sahib*.

2. The *Mulmantra* contains the basic tenet of Sikh belief and the Sikh's Gur-mantra is Waheguru

3. Daily recite the five *Banis* namely, *Japji, Jaap, Swayyas, Rehras-chaupai* and *Kirtan-Sohila*.

4. Maintenance of the Five Ks: *Kesh, Kirpan, Kachh, Kara and Kanga.*

5. No stealing, plundering, gambling or exploitation of the poor.

6. No coveting of another's wealth or wife.

7. No use of intoxicants like wine, hemp, opium, toddy etc.

8. Do not commit any religious offence (Kurahit) like the removal of hair, the use of tobacco, eating *Halal* meat or adultery. If a Khalsa does any of these, he has to take the *Amrit* again, after due penance.

9. Do not perform any Hindu or other ritualisitic ceremonies on occasions of birth, marriage or death in the family. Only Sikh ceremonies are to be performed.

10. Follow no rituals such as *Havans, Pitries* (ancestor-feeding), worship of idols or of graves, tombs, monasteries or *maths*.

11. Have no relationships with Minas, Dhir-malias, Ramrais and Massands.

In addition to the above instructions, Guru Gobind Singh also gave oral instructions to well-known Khalsa-leaders like Bhai Daya Singh, Bhai Desa Singh, Bhai Chaupa Singh. These were later written down and were called *Rahat-Namas* (Codes of conduct). He also gave some instructions to Bhai Nand Lal, the poet-laureate of his court, which is called *Tankhah-Nama*. The main points of these instructions are given below:

(i) A Khalsa should not follow any ascetic practices of Yogis, Sanyasis etc. and should not follow any Tantra, Mantra or Jantra.

(ii) He should not give his daughter in marriage to a *Patit* Sikh or accept any money for the marriage of his daughter from the boy's family.

(iii)   He should give one-tenth of his income to charitable or religious puposes.

(iv)   He should not wear a cap, hat or helmet.

(v)   He should not use any money from temple-offerings or charity funds. If he happens to be a priest, a *granthi* or the caretaker of a *Gurdwara*, he should accept only what is necessary for his needs.

(vi)   He should marry within the Sikh Panth.

(vii)   He should not break his vows or any other promise he makes nor commit perjury or treachery.

(viii) He should not listen to vulgar, profane or sexy songs.

(ix)   He should have his head covered whenever going out.

(x)   He should teach his children how to read the *Guru Granth Sahib* and understand its contents.

(xi)   He should use the Sikh greeting when greeting another Sikh, namely *Waheguru ji ka Khalsa Waheguru ji ki Fateh.*

The above instructions form the main part of the Code of Discipline. They may be catagorised under two headings: religious and social. The religious directives are in keeping with the Sikh tradition. The social directives are intended to make the Khalsa a good citizen and a responsible member of the community. The prohibition of theft, plunder, perjury, treachery, cheating, gambling and exploitation of the poor and weak sections of the community contribute to the smoothening of the course of normal social life and benefit the community as a whole. The bans on the use of alcohol and tobacco are intended to safeguard the health of the Khalsa. The Directives against the four misdemeanours, association with *patits*, Dhirmalias etc., the misuse of religious offerings and charities, are meant to wean the Khalsa from religious misdeeds. All in all, the code is intended to make a Khalsa an ideal person.

67. Is holy congregation (Satsang) necessary?

In Sikhism, great emphasis is laid on *Satsang*. By joining congregational prayers and making contact with saints the devotee comes to divine knowledge. The inspiration given by good people leads to the development of the spiritual personality. Holy people preach purity through personal example and kindle the heart with universal love. They warn the individual of the five great vices. Psychologically, the association with holy men helps as a deterrent against evil thoughts and deeds. Just as a tree which grows near a sandalwood tree acquires the fragrance of sandal, just as a metal when touched with the philosopher's stone is transmuted into gold so in the same way, an ordinary man becomes ennoble and heroic in the company of holy men. In the company of The Truthful, a devotee learns the value of "The Truth".

Joining the company of saints, is also conducive to the discipline of the mind. One learns how to serve the community and work for the good of humanity. One acquires the technique of "The Name" and so comes to enjoy inner tranquility. According to Guru Nanak, "The company of saints is also the school of the Guru, where one learns Godly attributes." There, evil is purged and destroyed, as if by a divine spark. Guru Arjan says, "The society of saints removes sin; the society of saints brings comforts in this world and the next."

Again and again, in the *Guru Granth Sahib*, a Sikh is required to seek the company of noble souls. A man is known by the company he keeps. In good company, he becomes good and sheds his evil tendencies. He will learn to be ashamed of doing anything which may bring him reproach.

Man's actions are so often motivated by the herd instinct. He does certain things as a matter of social convention, if his society becomes an instrument of his progress, he can rise to greater heights. For this reason, the Sikh in his general prayer—the *Ardas*—seeks the company of the holy and to contact virtuous men—*Sadh ka sung, Gurmukh da mel.*

68. How should we treat the apostates—Patits?

The weak followers of any religion are likely to renounce their faith in fear or temptation, so it is, necessary to accept only those adherents who have a firm and sincere belief in the basic tenets of their religion.

It has been observed that some Sikhs become apostates—*Patits*—on account of mixing with bad company, when they go to foreign countries. Some people have told me that they shaved because otherwise they could not get employment. This is not always true, because some *Keshadhari* Sikhs are able to get decent jobs. It all depends on the qualifications of the individual Sikh. Some Sikhs may have shaved because they mixed with foreign girls and wanted to appear more acceptable to them, like so many things, a reflection of their human weakness.

Much depends on the strength and vitality of the individual's faith. Recently, a Sikh bus-conductor in England won the right to wear a turban on duty. Another Sikh who was not admitted to a recreation club received an apology from the management. If the Sikhs in the West maintain their form and symbols, the turban and the beard will become respected. Recently the Sikhs in Britain won the right of riding motorcycles with turbans instead of helmets. Similarly Sikhs with turbans have been allowed to join the U.S. Navy.

The reclamation of apostates should be given the greatest encouragement in any programme of spiritual uplift. The apostates have to be persuaded to realise their shortcomings and weaknesses and convinced of the value of repentance and the turning over of a new leaf.

According to the *Rahtnama*, the Khalsa must maintain his tradition and individuality:

"So long as the Khalsa remains distinct,

His glory and lustre will grow,

Once he adopts Brahmanical ways

It will not be possible to trust him."

Many apostates, in their heart of hearts, realise that they have wronged themselves and their community, but do not have the moral courage to admit to their weakness. The only approach to *Patits* is to re-educate them and offer assistance in their return to the Sikh fold. Give understanding and sympathy, they may well react favourably to an approach by responsible Sikhs.

69. Are there castes among the Sikhs?

Five hundred years ago, Guru Nanak introduced the concept of a casteless society. The Hindus rigidly adhered to the caste system which divided the community into water-tight compartments. This not only prevents social intercourse but also encourages fatalism.

According to Guru Nanak, no man is born high or low. Taking the image of the potter's wheel, Guru Arjan compared the different kinds of people to vessels of many types and patterns, but all made of clay. In spite of religious and social distinctions, all mankind is of one basic material common to all.

Many Indian saints and *Bhagats** belonged to low castes, but this did not stand in the way of their spiritual attainment. They are still revered and worshipped on account of their saintliness. God's Name burns away all impurities and ennobles the individual.

According to Guru Nanak, caste is humbug. He writes: "From one Light the whole world came into being; so, who is good and who is bad?" Caste is man made division for selfish ends. According to Hinduism, one belonging to the lowest caste was not even regarded as worthy of religious instruction. Moreover, birth determined status and this could not be changed. This was against the Guru's basic belief in the right of every individual, to the opportunity for both social and spiritual uplift.

A man becomes high or low according to his actions. Only they are really depressed who forget the Lord. When Guru Nanak was asked about his own caste, he replied. "I belong to the lowest among the low castes." Kabir challenged the Brahmins and inquired if they were not born in the same way as men of the so-called low castes. Moreover, caste is of no consequence in the next world, or in the court of God.

Any consideration of caste in matters of matrimony should be discouraged. Caste distinctions were abolished by Guru Gobind Singh. When a disciple becomes a Khalsa, he renounces his previous caste and becomes a member of a casteless society:

"The caste of all mankind is one and the same".

70. What is the basic creed of the Sikhs?

The basic creed of the Sikhs—The *Mul Mantra*—gives the idea of Reality in a few telling words. The creed is: *Ekonkar Satnam, Karta Purkh, Nirbhav, Nirvair, Akal Murat, Ajoni, Suabhav, Gur Parsad*. In these words, Guru Nanak praises God and mentions some of His great attributes: He is Truth, Self-created, beyond the limits of time, He can be realised

---

*Bhagats: Saints or seers.

through the grace of the Guru. Let us study the meaning of each word of the *Mul Mantra*.

(a) *Ekonkar*: The only One Absolute God who is forever unfolding. He is the Absolute—the Transcendental. As such, He is Unknowable, Unfathomable. He is beyond description and beyond human comprehension.

(b) *Satnam*: His name is true. He really exists. He is not an idea or a hypothesis or an illusion. As one who exists, He is ever changing. He is never the same, evolving and growing. Everything exists in Him and is caused by Him. His name is Truth. He is formless—He is "The Holy spirit"—NAM.

(c) *Karta Purkh*: He is the Creator of the cosmos. He is responsible for the coming into existence of the whole universe.

(d) *Nirbhav*: He is fearless. He is afraid of no one because He is the Lord of the universe.

(e) *Nirvair*: He is without any enmity. His love and protection extend to all. This cuts at the root of the theory of the chosen prophets and the chosen people. Like God, a true Sikh must be fearless and impartial. This will help to establish equality and justice.

(f) *Akal Murat*: He is Timeless. He is not subject to death.

(g) *Ajoni*: He is unborn. God does not take birth in any manner. This is the very antithesis of the theory of incarnation.

(h) *Suabhav*: He is self-existent. He is unique in His own right.

(i) *Gur Prasad*: By the grace of the Guru, the Sikh can acquire knowledge of God.

The short from of the creed is *Ekonkar Satgur Prashad* as used in the Guru Granth Sahib.

71. What is the Temple of Bread (Langar)?

The institution of "free kitchen" or the "temple of bread", as Puran Singh called it, was started by Guru Nanak. He desired that every Sikh should share his food with others—*Wand Chhakna*—and that his kitchen should be open to all. Subsequently the *Langar* took on an institution form and became a part of the Sikh temple. This community kitchen is meant to provide food to all devotees and pilgrims. Every Sikh is expected to contribute to it either by donating food stuff or by participating in the cooking and distribution of the food.

Guru Nanak set up a temple of bread at Kartar Pur where people brought corn and fuel, and worked together to prepare a common meal for the whole community. Guru Angad extended the Langar and personally served in it. Guru Amardas turned it into an institution and ordered that all who came to see him must first eat in *Langar*: food first, congregation next—*pahlay pangat, peechay sangat*. Even the Emperor Akbar and the Raja of Haripur had to sit on the floor with the common people and take a meal with them. Apart from promoting social equality, the *Langar* eliminated taboos about *chauka*—the preparation of food in special enclosures etc. The scope of "*Langar*" was widened by Guru Ram das who ordered that water and meals be also served to travellers and squatters. Guru Arjan and his wife personally served water to the *Sangat*. They even massaged the weary travellers and fanned them to sleep.

Many of the Sikhs started their own *Langars* at Anandpur. One day, Guru Gobind Singh went out *incognito* on an inspection of *Langars*. He found out that Bhai Nandlal maintained the *Langar* well, while others were indifferent to the needs of poor Sikhs. He warned them and remarked: "The mouths of the poor are Guru's receptacles of gifts."

According to Prof. Puran Singh, "What is a home but a hospitable feasting of children with bread, love and faith?" What is spiritual life in a temple of flesh without a full meal first? The very first temple made by Guru Nanak therefore, was the Temple of Bread or Guru's *Langar*.

72. What is the scope of the comprehensive discipline in a Sikh's life?

In his personal life, a true Sikh has to follow a three-fold discipline: the discipline of the Word, the discipline of the Sacrament and the discipline of Service.

The discipline of The *Word* implies that the Sikhs must rise early in the morning, say at about 4 a.m., take a bath and then meditate on The Name. He has to read daily the five *Banis: Japji, Jap Sahib, ten Swayyas, Rahras* and *Kirtan Sohila*. He should visit the Gurdwara daily. If possible, he must sing hymns and read from the Guru Granth Sahib.

The discipline of the *sacrament* implies that the Sikh must follow the Sikh ceremonies at the time of birth, marriage and death. On all such occasions, he must conduct himself with dignity and equipoise and offer prayers suitable to the occasion.

The discipline of *"Service"* requires that the Sikh must serve his fellow-men to demonstrate his love of God. In the sphere of service, barriers of caste or creed or race must be ignored. Gurdwaras are places for service to the *Sangat*. A Sikh may sweep the floor, cleanse the utensils, polish the shoes or serve water. *Langar* provides an extensive field of service. A Sikh may contribute food-stuff and provisions, pay for fuel or utensils, fetch water or lend a helping hand in the cooking and distribution of food.

In corporate life, a Sikh is expected to do his duty to the community. He should take *Amrit* (Baptism) and encourage others to do the same. He should join the congregation—*Sangat,* and assist any *Panthic* meeting to arrive at decisions—Gurmata. He should also readily submit to disciplinary action in case of misdeeds or acts of indiscipline. In short, he should take an active part in the corporate life of the *Panth*. Such a Sikh earns the Guru's grace.

73. What is the routine of a Sikh?

Practical Sikhism is based on three pragmatic concepts *Nam japna, Kirt Karna and Wand Chhakna*. This three-fold path signifies the remembrance of "The Name" performing honest labour for a living and sharing one's earnings with others. All is to be practised in daily life.

Guru Amardas advised Bhai Buddha regarding an ideal Sikh's life. Some of the points are mentioned below:

A Sikh should serve the people and not touch money or property belonging to others. Let him share his joys and sorrows with his neighbours. He should eat only when he feels hungry and sleep only when he feels sleepy.

Let him resign himself to the Will of God and never find fault with any doings of his Creator. He should keep away from lust, anger and greed, not boast of his goodness or kindness. He shall practise charity and personal cleanlines. He should not tolerate any irreverence towards the Gurus. In short, let him mould his life and conduct according to the Guru's teachings.

Guru Ramdas laid down the following routine for a true Sikh. Let the Sikh get up at dawn and after bathing, meditate on the Divine Name and continue his meditation till sunrise. Then go out to earn his daily bread by honest means. Let his calling or work be such that it keeps him away from unfair and untruthful means. Let him repeat "The Name" or *Gurbani* while working or walking. After his day's work, let him again offer prayers before retiring for the night. The Guru seeks the dust of the feet of those who remember God's Name and who also encourage others to repeat "The Name".

The recommended pattern of life is that of a householder: *Grahast-mai-udas*. The devotee should learn to remain contented and desireless while leading his life as a citizen. Let him raise himself above worldly temptation and become a model for others. With the Guru's Grace, he will lead a pious and clean life. It is a great advantage to maintain a diary of one's daily actions. Such a practice will deter one from bad deeds. Moreover, whenever convenient one should join the *Sadh Sangat* for *Kirtan* and *Katha*. Man amasses the dust of sin through numerous lives, his cleaning process will also be a long and arduous one.

74. How can a man turn towards God?

Though it is not possible for man to become God, he may try to become God-like. According to Guru Arjan, there is no difference between the God-conscious soul and God.

A man of God may lead the life of a householder or an ascetic. He has to observe strict physical, moral and spiritual discipline. He is not affected by the five deadly sins of lust, anger, greed, attachment or pride. He speaks the truth and leads a pure life. He is indifferent to pain or pleasure, praise or blame. He is humble and weak in spirit. He loves to serve all human beings, birds and beasts. He sees God in all sentient and non-sentient objects.

The true devotee, to progress God-ward, must have complete faith in God. He should minimise his attachment to worldly desire. He should associate with holy people. He should always be ready to sacrifice everything and submit himself to the Will of God. He is not afraid of pain or suffering, when it comes from God. Suffering purifies the soul and makes it worthy to merit union with the Almighty.

The devotee must aspire to true knowledge. Acquiring a knowledge of the truth and practical true living are very important. He should engage whenever it is possible in meditation on "The Name": and think of God all the time.

A man of God does not remain idle or indifferent to another's suffering. He engages himself in acts of love and charity. He feels happy in doing good to others. This helps in the elimination of selfishness and egoism.

An anchorite must keep clear of any temptations and pitfalls. For this, control over the mind is necessary.

Man in his period of human life should practise holiness so that he may ultimately unite with God and be free from the cycle of birth and death, Guru Arjan says:

"Fix your attention upon the Almighty and you may obtain honour at His Court".

Such persons enjoy the companionship of God at all times.

75. Is drinking permitted in Sikhism?

The Sikh Gurus banned the use of intoxicants including alcohol on account of its harmful effects. It is physically harmful and mentally disturbing. Man, under the influence of drink, loses the power to reason and normal action. Guru Amardas wrote in the Guru Granth Sahib (p. 554) against the use of wine by the Sikhs.

"One man offers wine and another pours it himself;

It makes him crazy and senseless and devoid of all reason.

Then one cannot distinguish between one's own and another's and is cursed by God.

Drinking it, one forsakes one's Master and is punished at the Lord's Court.

Yes, drink not this vicious wine, under any circumstances."

At another place the Guru wrote that the wages of drinking are sin and vice (p. 553);

"The body is the pitcher, selfhood the wine;

And society is of craving and outgoing of the mind.

Yes, Desire is drinking bowl brimming over with falsehood;

And *Yama* is the bar-man.

Drinking such a wine, who can earn anything but vice and sin?"

Guru Gobind Singh in his *Rahatnama* addressed to Bhai Chaupa Singh banned the use of any intoxicating drink. A Sikh of the Guru should never drink wine. (*Guru Ka Sikh Sharab Kadi Na Peevay*).

Apart from religious injunction, scientists have proved that the frequent use of alcohol makes people addicts and they become aggressive and unruly. The custom of offering drinks to friends and guests is socially dangerous. And when taken in excess can have terrible effects on one's general health.

Drinking damages the liver, the heart and the brain. In the United States of America "alcoholism" is regarded as a disease to be controlled by society and government.

In Persian language, wine is called *Sharaab* which literally means 'the water of mischief."

Let all Sikhs clearly understand that drinking is under no circumstances permitted in Sikh religion. The clear command in Sri Guru Granth Sahib and *Rehat Maryada* bans the use of any intoxicants by any Sikh.

Kabir says in the *Adi Granth:*

"Whoever uses *bhang*, fish and wine;

Whatever pilgrimages, fastings and daily rites they may perform,
They all go to hell." (p. 1377).

76. What is the attitude of Sikh Faith towards non-vegetarian food?

The general directive of Guru Nanak with regard to food is: "Do not take that food which effects health, causes pain or suffering to the body or produces evil thoughts in the mind". (p. 16). There is a close connection between body and the mind so that the food that we eat affects both of them. Guru Ramdas has mentioned the three qualities created by God. These are *Rajas* (Activity or motion), *Tamas* (Resistance or darkness), *Satav* (Harmony or goodness). He says:

"God Himself created the three qualities and increased our love for worldly valuables" (p. 1237). Food can also be categorised under these three qualities. For example, fresh and natural food is an example of Satav, fried and spicy food is of *Rajas,* while fermented, decomposed, preserve or frozen food is a kind of *Tamas.* If one eats heavy or spicy food, one's stomach easily gets upset. Over-eating and heavy food should be avoided. Simple and natural food is best for healthy living.

There are references to matter of food in the *Adi Granth.* If one believes that all creation is a manifestation of God, the destruction of any living being or micro-organism is an infringement of the natural right to live. Kabir says:

"If you say that God resides in all, why do you kill a hen?" (A.G., p, 1350). Kabir favours a vegetarian diet.

He says:

"It is foolish to kill animals by cruelty and call it sanctified food." (p. 1375.)

"You kill life and call it an act of religion. Then what is irreligion?" (p. 1103). Though unnecessary killing or causing suffering to animals and birds for the sake of providing human food is to be avoided, vegetarianism should not be turned into a phobia or dogma.

Undoubtedly, animal food is largely used for satisfying the human palate. To eat meat only for the satisfaction of one's taste or appetite is not good. Kabir says, "You keep fasts in order to become acceptable to God, but kill a living animal for your relish". (p. 483). This refers to the eating of meat by Muslims after breaking the religious fast.

The Gurus did not like the taboo on meat when more important things like control over desires or passion were ignored. It is far more important to kill the evil that pollutes the mind rather than abstain from meat. Impurities of the mind should be removed first, before labelling some food as pure and the other impure.

There is a passage in the *Guru Granth Sahib* which indicates the futility of the controversy regarding vegetarian and non-vegetarian food. It is said that when the Brahmins of Kurukshetra advocated the need and benefit of vegetarian food, Guru Nanak replied to them as under:

"Only the foolish quarrel over the desirability of eating flesh. They are oblivious of true knowledge and meditation. What is really flesh? What is really vegetable-food? Which one of is sin-infested?

They do not differentiate between good food and that which leads to sin.......

Men are born of a mother's and father's blood yet they do not eat fish or meat.......

Meat is mentioned in the Puranas and the Katebas:

It has been used in Yajnas on marriages and festive occasions". (p. 1290). Equally fruitless is the debate on the question whether fish or eggs are included in non-vegetarian diet or not.

The Gurus neither advocated meat nor banned its use. They left it to the choice of the individual. There are passages against meat, in the *Guru Granth Sahib*. Guru Gobind Singh however prohibited for the Khalsa the use of *Halal* or *Kutha* meat prepared in the Muslim ritualistic way. It may be noted that by tradition, meat is never served in the *Guru Ka Langar* (Free Kitchen).

Vegetarianism by itself cannot confer spiritual merit or lead to the door of salvation. Spiritual achievement depends on *Sadhana* or religious discipline. However, it has been observed by many saints that a vegetarian diet does help in *Sadhana*. Guru Amardas says:

"Those who take dirty food increase their filth; such filth causes sorrow to the egocentric person". (p. 121).

The position with regard to the meat of the cow or beef, is that the Sikhs do not venerate the cow like the Hindus. The latter view the cow as a mother, because she supplies milk to the child when the mother's milk fails. However, beef is not taboo for the Sikhs as *Halal* is. A non-vegetarian Sikh can take beef or pork as readily as any other meat. For those who want to advance on the spiritual path, vegetarian food is generally recommended by holy men as it avoids the killing of animals and birds.

IV. Sikh History

77. What was the mission of Guru Nanak?

Guru Nanak was born in Talwandi, a village in Punjab, in 1469 at a critical period of Indian history. The Lodi rulers wallowed in luxury and did not care for the affairs of State and welfare of their subjects. Their weakness and sloth brought Babar on to the Indian scene. Guru Nanak protested against foreign domination and warned the rulers that if they did not look into the grievances of the people, they would meet the punishment they deserved.

Guru Nanak challenged the fanaticism and intolerance of the Muslims, of his time. During his visit to Mecca, he made the *Kazis* realise that God's house is everywhere and not only in the direction of the *Kaaba*. Similarly, Guru Nanak also exposed the meaningless ritual and caste prejudices prevalent among the Hindus. He demonstrated to them the fallacy of feeding Brahmins at the time of the performance of the *Sharaadha*. At Hardwar, in a very amusing way, he exposed the folly of offering water to the manes of ancestors.

Guru Nanak's life may be divided into three parts. The first period of 30 years was spent at Talwandi and Sultanpur as a householder. The second period of 22 years was spent in missionary travels far and wide and for the third and last period of 18 years he stayed at Kartarpur for the benefit of his followers. He established places of worship called *Dharamsalas*. Wherever he went, he urged people to perform acts of charity and render services to the poor and the needy.

Guru Nanak propagated the equality of man. He treated Hindus and Muslims alike. He went to their important shrines and explained to them the true way of spiritual life. He opposed the distinctions of caste. He called himself a member of the lowest caste.

Guru Nanak insisted on *Grahstha*—living a house-holder's life. The path of renunciation or *Sanyas* is the way of escapism and defeat. Man must do his worldly duties and at the same time keep his spirit detached from worldly things.

Finding that his end was approaching, Guru Nanak tested his disciples and passed *Gurudom* onto the most worthy of them, Guru Angad, in 1539.

78. What do you know of Guru Angad?

Guru Angad (1504-52) previously known as Lehna was a worshipper of the goddess Jawala Mukhi. Once, while going to the shrine of this goddess, he came in contact with Guru Nanak. There was spontaneous conversion. He chose to serve the Guru. He became the Guru's best and obedient follower. After testing him along with others, Guru Nanak nominated him to the *Gaddi* in 1539.

Guru Angad popularised the *Gurmukhi* script introduced by Guru Nanak. He broke the Brahmin's monopoly of learning by encouraging all sorts of people to learn *Gurmukhi* (the Guru's script) and read religious literature. He gathered the facts about Guru Nanak's life from Bhai Bala and wrote the first biography of Guru Nanak Dev. He also set up religious centres where the principles of Sikhism could be propagated.

Guru Angad extended *Langar*—the free kitchen—and personally looked after the serving arrangements. *Langar* was intended to break caste barriers and social taboos.

Guru Angad laid stress on the equality of man:

"It is like clay from which pots are made

In diverse shapes and forms—yet the clay is the same. Similarly the bodies of men are made from the same five elements, so

How can one amongst them, be high and the other low?"

Langar made people of different castes sit in line on the same platform and so provided a healthy forum for charity and service.

Guru Angad was very fond of children. He started a school for young boys and taught them the *Gurmukhi* script. He also insisted on physical fitness. He opened a gymnasium which had a wrestling arena, rural sports and games followed religious congregations. This tradition subsequently helped in enlisting able-bodied men for the Sikh army.

Guru Angad led a life of piety and service at Khadur. Here Amardas— a relative of his—served him day and night. The Guru bypassed his sons, who were disobedient and nominated Amardas as his successor in 1552.

79. What do you know of Guru Amardas?

Guru Amardas (1479—1574) came to the succession by dint of his selfless services, at the age of 73. Guru Angad's son, Dattu, was enraged at this and kicked Guru Amardas. Guru Amardas did not take it ill but rather apologised to him, saying "Pardon me; my hard bones must have hurt your foot." Thus reflecting the Guru's great humility and wisdom.

Guru Amardas paid serious attention to the propagation of Sikhism. He appointed a devout Sikh in charge of each region. The total number of such diocese were 22. The Guru also trained a number of travelling missionaries who spread the message of Sikhism to other parts of India. In order to bring the Sikhs closer to one another he fixed three festivals— Diwali, Baisakhi and Maghi—when all could assemble for religious conference.

It is said that the followers of Sri Chand, son of Guru Nanak who had started the Udasi group and who had advocated the rununciation of home and property, came to Guru Amardas for consultation. The Guru advised them to lead a life of renunciation in the midst of the home. He explained it was a compromise between asceticism and worldly enjoyment. The householder's life was indeed the best life, because, it offered an easy way for the common man—Remembrance of God, sharing of food and income, and honest living—Nam japna, Wand chhakna and Dharam-di-kirt. The Guru started a new centre of worship at Goindwal where he dug a well for the benefit of the people.

Guru Amardas was very friendly to the emperor Akbar. The Emperor came to pay respects to Guru Amardas at Goindwal and according to custom took meals in the Langar. He was very much impressed by the universal message of Sikhism and its free kitchen.

Guru Amardas, in the tradition of Guru Nanak, tested his disciples before nominating a successor. He found in his son-in-law, Bhai Jetha, a devoted and humble Sikh. He, therefore, installed him as Guru Ramdas in 1574.

80. What do you know of Guru Ramdas?

Guru Ramdas (1534—1581) was installed as Guru at the age of forty. He put missionary work on sound basis and sent massands to different parts of north India to propagate the message of Sikhism. He himself was fond of serving his disciples. Sometimes, he would distribute water or pull the fan for the *Sangat*.

Guru Ramdas was keen on giving a suitable centre of worship to the Sikhs. He developed the land purchased from local land owners and established a new township called Ramdaspur. Many Sikhs settled in the new town because it was situated on the trade routes. The city was subsequently called Amritsar.

Guru Ramdas was a perfect example of humility and piety. Once Sri Chand—the son of Guru Nanak—visited him. He asked the Guru in a humorous way as to why he maintained a long and flowing beard. The Guru gave him an apt reply: "To wipe the dust of your holy feet." Sri Chand was deeply moved by this answer and expressed regret for his impertinence.

The Guru's mission spread quickly among the poor and rich classes. Some aristocrats visited Amritsar and became his followers. The Guru turned his friendship with Emperor Akbar to good account by persuading him to relieve distress and to remove the oppressive taxes on non-Muslims.

Guru Ramdas laid down a Sikh code of conduct and worship. He prescribed the routine of a Sikh as in his hymn to be found on page 305 of *Guru Granth Sahib*. He composed the *Lavan* for Sikh marriage cermony and other hymns appropriate to certain other functions and festivities. Being a talented musician he composed hymns in eleven new ragas.

Arjan, the youngest son of Guru Ramdas was devoted to his father. At the bidding of his father, he went to Lahore to attend a marriage. He was feeling terribly depressed without his father. He wrote two urgent poetic letters, full of longing and love for the Guru.

"My soul yearns for the sight of the Guru.

It bewails like the *Chatrik* crying for the rain." (A.G. p. 96).

These letters were intercepted by his elder brother Prithi Chand. When the third letter reached Guru Ramdas, he immediately called him. Prithi Chand was keen on the succession, but the Guru tested his sons and finally his choice fell on Arjan who was installed as the Fifth Guru in 1581.

81. What do you know of Guru Arjan?

Guru Arjan (1563—1606) was in his teens when he was installed as Guru. He developed Amritsar as a centre of industry and culture for the Sikhs. He requested Mian Mir—a Muslim divine—to lay the foundation stone of the *Har Mandar* (Temple of God). The temple was built on a level lower than the surrounding land, in the middle of a beautiful lake. This is now known as the Golden Temple.

In order to put the township on a sound basis, the Guru helped the establishment of new trades and professions. Some of these trades were banking, embroidery, carpentry and horse trading. Amritsar was centrally situated and there was enough scope for commercial relations with neighbouring countries. The Sikhs were sent to Afghanistan and Central Asia for buying good horses. The trade in horses gave Sikhs a taste for riding and horsemanship.

Guru Arjan felt that the Sikhs should have their own scripture. He collected the hymns of the first four Gurus and of Indian *Bhagats* and *Bhatts*. He dictated the hymns including his own to Bhai Gurdas and completed the compilation of the *Adi Granth* the first book in 1604.

Guru Arjan was a man of the pople and wielded great influence. His growing power and prestige aroused the jealousy of Emperor Jahangir. Even Muslims came to the *Har Mandar*. Jahangir resolved, to use his own words, "to put an end to this traffic." He asked Guru Arjan to change the text of part of his Granth to include the praise of the prophet Mohammed. The Guru refused to do so. In the meantime, Chandu—the Diwan—who bore a grudge against the Guru—poisoned the mind of Jahangir with all sorts of false stories. Jahangir placed Guru Arjan in the charge of Chandu. The latter perpetrated tortures like pouring boiling water on him, throwing burning sand on the Guru. Guru Arjan bore all these tortures with great resignation.

After nominating his son Har Gobind as his successor, the Guru was taken to the river bank. His body was then thrown into the river as a final torture. He is the first martyr in Sikh history.

82. What do you know of Guru Har Gobind?

Guru Har Gobind (1595-1644) acted as per the advice of his father to maintain an army. His father had been a victim of Mughal tyranny. The

Mughal rulers wanted to break the power of the Sikhs. He organised a band of soldiers and trained them in warfare. Some historians call it the beginning of a military theocracy power of the Sikhs. He organised a band of soldiers and trained them in warfare. Some historians call it the Emperor Jahangir felt jealous of the Guru's military power and had him imprisoned in Gwalior fort. When the Guru's release was ordered, he refused to leave the fort till the other Indian princes who were also in jail were released. After this was done the Guru came to be known, as *Bandhichhor* or the Great Liberator. Indian princes who were also in jail were released. After this was done the Guru came to be known as *Bandhichhor* or the Great Liberator.

Guru Har Gobind realised that a fight with the Mughal power was inevitable, so he had his small army well trained. He himself was a great rider, hunter and swordsman. Cunningham reports that he had 800 horses, 300 trained horsemen and 60 artillery-men. Guru Har Gobind fought three major battles which were forced on him by the Mughals. The first battle at Amritsar was fought in 1634. The Commander of the Mughals-Mukhlis Khan was completely routed. In the second battle near Lehra in 1637, the Guru's army was also victorious. The third battle in which Painde Khan got killed was fought at Kartarpur in 1638. The Guru's success in all the three battles created confidence and inspried courage among his Sikhs.

Guru Har Gobind's career marks the turning point in Sikh history. Due to the new circumstances, Sikhism was becoming militant. The Guru carried two swords; one of spiritual power-*Peeri*, and the other of military power-*Meeri*. The Sikhs had challenged the Mughal power, and has raised the banner of revolt against a cruel and corrupt administration. The martydom of Guru Arjan had not been in vain. The mission of the Sikhs henceforth was for the liberation of people from religious and political typranny. The use of the sword as means of defence and justice became popular among the Guru's followers. In 1644, Guru Har Gobind nominated Guru Har Rai as his successor.

83. What do you know of Guru Har Rai?

83. Guru Har Rai (1630-1661) was installed as Guru at the age of 14. He was the grandson of Guru Har Gobind though without his military genius. Guru Har Rai was a man of peace and love. He was fond of serving the *Sangat.* He urged his followers to meditate on the hymns of the Guru Granth Sahib and to lead a life of self-discipline.

Guru Har Rai tried to isolate himself from the intrigues of the

Mughal court. Dara Shikoh came to the Guru's place and sought his blessing for success against his brother Aurangzeb. As was the tradition of the Gurus, Har Rai helped him in his distress as he would have helped any other man in difficulties. Aurangzeb captured Dara and had him executed. Emperor Aurngzeb then called the Guru to his court in connection with his alleged assistance to Dara. The Guru sent his son Ram Rai to the Mughal court. There, he worked miracles and even changed the text of a line of the *Granth* to please the Emperor. Guru Har Rai was so completely displeased with Ram Rai on this account that he disowned him.

Guru Har Rai was a man of great charity and generosity. Once, the ancstors of the former rulers of Patiala, Nabha and Jind came to the Guru's *Darbar*, crying for food and pattting their bellies in token of hunger. The Guru took pity on them and blessed them. Soon thereafter, they acquired territories and became Rajahs.

Guru Har Rai loved his devotees and helped them in times of need. One day Bhai Gobind of Kabul was so engrossed in his meditation on the Guru that he held him love-fettered for the whole day. Similarly, one morning the Guru spontaneously went to the house of an old pious lady who had prepared loaves of bread for him with great devotion. Knowing that his end was near, the Guru installed his five-year old son Harkrishan as the next Guru, early in October, 1661.

84. What do you know of Guru Harkrishan?

Guru Harkrishan (1656-1664) was called upon to assume the responsibilites of leadership of the Sikh community at the tender age of five. He is known as the "Child Guru" and is specially loved and cherished by children and students.

Guru Harkrishan was a genius and showed extraordinary talents for his age. Once a Brahmin questioned him about the meaning of certain difficult passages in the *Gita*. He wanted to test the intellectual powers of the Guru.The Guru did not take it ill and called a passing unlettered wateer-carrier to expound the meaning of those passages. The Brahmin was surprised at the extraordinary exposition and wisdom of the water-carrier. A Gurdwara known as "Panjokhra Sahib" was later established at this spot.

Once Raja Jai Singh decided to seek and then test out the genius and wisdom of the child Guru. He disguised his queen as a slave and made her sit among many other women in the Guru's presence. He asked the Guru to point out which was the queen. By his extraordinary talent the Guru went directly to the queen and sat on her lap. The Raja became a devoted disciple of the Guru.

The Guru's elder brother Ram Rai complained to Emperor Aurangzeb that he had been passed over for the succession. He claimed the right of succession as the eldest son of Guru Har Rai. The emperor called Guru Harkrishan to Delhi. In response at the wishes of the *Sangat*, the Guru went to Delhi and while there started his mission of healing the sick. Cholera was raging in the capital at that time. The Guru brought health and happiness to many Cholera-stricken people. The Guru stayed at the place where Gurdwara Bangla Sahib now stands. Soon after, he fell ill. Asked about his successor, he gave a cryptic reply: *"Baba Bakale."* He meant that the next Guru would be found in the village of Bakala. He passed away on 30th March, 1664.

85. What do you now of Guru Tegh Bahadur?

Guru Harkrishan had not specifically named the Ninth Guru. So no less than 22 imposters who called themselves *Guru* set themselves up in the village of Bakala. Bhai Makhan Shah, a *Lubana* went to Bakala to discover the real Guru, thereby personal testimony, he discovered Guru Tegh Bahadur and proclaimed him as the Ninth Guru in 1664.

Guru Tegh Bahadur's life (1621-1675) may be divided into three periods: the first period of 23 years spent at Amritsar along with his father, the second period of 19 years was spent in quiet meditation at Bakala and the third period of 11 years he travelled exclusively in eastern India and then the Punjab.

Dhirmal, a nephew of Guru Tegh Bahadur was extremely jealous of and angry with the Guru. He wanted to kill the Guru. So he sent a number of dacoits to plunder the Guru's house. Sihan one of them, shot the Guru and injured his shoulder. The next morning, the Sikhs captured Sihan and brought him to the temple. The Guru pardoned him and set him free. The Guru said, "Forgiveness is a great virtue."

Some Kashmiri Hindus who were being forced to accept Islam came to Guru Tegh Bahadur at Anandpur. The Guru agreed to sacrifice his life for the protection of the Hindus . The Hindu pandits sent a message to Emperor Aurnagzeb that if Guru Tegh Bahadur accepted Islam, they would follow his example.

Emperor Aurangzeb ordered the imprisonment of Guru Tegh Bahadur. He told him either to accept Islam or to show a miracle. The Guru refused to do either. With regard to the performance of a miracle the Guru said "Is it not a great miracle that the emperor forgets his own death, while inflicting it on others?"

Aurangzeb ordered the Guru's execution. The executioner Adam Shah dealt the blow after the Guru had finished a recitation of *"Japji."* The head of the Guru fell into the lap of a Sikh who took it to Anandpur. The body was cremated by a Lubana Sikh at the place where now stands Gurdwara Rakabganj. Guru Tegh Bahadur's martyrdom is unique, he gave his life not for the preservation of Sikhism, but to protect the Hindu religion. His was the second martyrdom in Sikh history.

86. What do you know of Guru Gobind Singh?

86. Guru Gobind Singh (1666-1708) was installed as the Tenth Guru at the age of nine, soon after the martyrdom of his father. He knew that difficult times were ahead, particularly the struggle against Mughal imperialism. He, therefore, made preparations to meet the Mughal challenge, by training his disciples in the art of warfare.

Guru Gobind Singh has four-fold achievement to his credit: (a) the crushing blow dealt to the Mughal power, (b) the creation of the Khalsa Panth, (c) the production of creative and martial literature, (d) the installation of the *Adi Granth* as the Guru Granth Sahib and the perpetual Guru for the Sikhs.

Guru Gobind Singh was a true patriot. He upheld the dignity of man and opposed the tryannny and fanaticism of Aurangzeb. Emperor Aurangzeb made no secret of spreading Islam by force. Guru Gobind Singh with his warriors had to fight on two fronts-against the hill Rajahs and the Mughal army. His victories in the battle of *Bhangani* (1687) and *Nadaun* (1689) undermined both the powers of the hill Rajahs and the Mughals. He sacrificed his four sons, wife and mother for the sake of upholding the cause of justice and freedom. Guru Gobind

Singh exposed the evil deeds of the emperor in a poetic letter to Aurangazeb, entitled *Zafarnama.*

The Guru was a literary giant and a patron of poets. The bards of his court composed epics and martial verses, to inspire the Sikhs to acts of glory and valour.

Guru Gobind Singh abolished the order of *massands*-missionaries, because of their misdeeds. He further ordered the end of personal Gurudom, and declared *Sri Guru Granth Sahib* as an eternal Guru.

The creation of the Khalsa Panth in 1699 was another feat of genius. He conceived the idea of raising an army from men belonging to the lower castes and regarded as weak and depressed. He in turn also had his disciples administer *Amrit* to him. Guru Gobind Singh died from a mortal wound inflicted by two Pathans in 1708. Later Gurdwara Abchal Nagar, was built by Maharaja Ranjit Singh at Nanded on the spot where the Guru departed his mortal life.

87. What do you know of Banda Singh?

Banda Singh (1670-1716) was born at Rajouri in Jammu State. He was known as Lachman Dev in his childhood. Soon after a hunt, he turned ascetic: A *Bairagi,* and took the name of Madho Das. He settled down at Nanded. He became a devotee of the Guru in September 1708 and sought his blessings. Guru Gobind Singh gave him a sword, five arrows, a flag and a battle drum and asked him to follow the five commandments mentioned below.

Remain a celibate: do not marry at all.

Speak the truth and act on it.

Serve and obey the Khalsa Panth.

Do not establish a new sect or have yourself set up as a king.

Be humble and not haughty.

Taking twenty-five Sikhs with him, Banda Singh proceeded to the Punjab to punish the ememies of the Khalsa Panth. He attached Samana in November 1709. Thereafter, Wazir Khan the Nawab of Sarhind was killed in the battle of Chaper Chiri on 12th May, 1710.

Banda Singh was crowned at Lohgarh and struck coins in the name of the Guru. He allowed his Muslim subjects to follow their religious customs and practices. Soon afterwards, he extended his sway over Pathankot.

The Mughal emperor was perturbed by the conquests of Banda Singh and sent a big army to crush him, Banda Singh was besieged at Gurdas Nangal. After an eight-month siege, he and his followers were captured on 7th December 1715.

Banda Singh was tortured to death on 7th June 1716. It is said that Banda Singh confessed that he deserved his fate for transgressing the commands of Guru Gobind Singh.

Banda Singh's challenge to the Mughal power showed that the Khalsa had broken the reputation of Mughal invincibility. Given another chance, they could perhaps lay the foundations of a Sikh empire. The opportunity came in 1799, when Ranjit Singh established Sikh rule in the Punjab.

88. What do you know of Maharaja Ranjit Singh?

Ranjit Singh (1780-1839) was a member of the Sukerchakia misal. From early childhood, he was fond of riding and hunting. Taking advantage of the unsettled conditions in the Punjab, he expelled Chet Singh of Bhangi misal from Lahore and crowned as *Maharaja*. He captured Amritsar in 1802 and thereafter assumed full sovereignty over petty chiefs of Malwa. He crossed the Sutlej for extension of his dominion but the chiefs of Jind and Kaithal appealed to the British for help against Ranjit Singh. The British made a treaty with Ranjit Singh in 1809, declaring the Sutlej river as his frontier. In 1818, Ranjit Singh annexed Multan and a year later, Kashmir lay at his feet. He proceeded northward and annexed Peshawar in 1834.

Ranjit Singh is known as the lion of the Punjab. He was a born soldier and administrator. Sir Lepal Griffin called him, "The beau ideal of a soldier, strong, spare, active, courageous and enduring". He had a lot of common sense and ruled his empire with justice and wisdom. It is surprising that he abolished the death penalty in those turbulent times. He was a very tolerant ruler; the publiic offices were held by Muslims, Sikhs and Hindus on equal terms. He picked men of ability and character for administration and encouraged budding talent. His royal court was cosmopolitan in character. He employed European officers to train his army on modern lines.

Ranjit Singh as a Sikh, created endowments for religious uses and alloted land to Hindu, Muslim and Sikh shrines for their upkeep. He was a strict disciplinarian and used to move in disguise to look after his subjects.

Ranjit Singh gave the Punjab a good and enlightened administration. He prohibited traffic in women and children. He patronised artists and warriors. He dispensed justice impartially. He was fond of the joys of life but never neglected public affairs for personal pleasure. It is significant that he gave a period of peace and efficient administration to the Punjab and checked the aggressive designs of the Briitish power in Northern India.

89. What do you know of Bhai Vir Singh?

Bhai Vir Singh (1872-1957) was the most important writer and theologian in Punjabi who expounded Sikh history and philosophy for more than fifty years. He is regarded as the Bhai Gurdas of the twentieth century. His most important works are *Guru Nanak Chamatkar, Kalgidhar Chamatkar, Baba Nodh Singh and Meray Saeeyan jeeo*.

Bhai Vir Singh's creative talent was recognised by the Government and the Punjab University. He was given the title of *Padam Shri* by the Goverment of India and a Honorary Doctorate by the Punjab University. H. Chattopadhaya called him the "sixth river in the land of the five rivers." His poetry possesses the sublimity of Milton, the spontaneity of Wordsworth, the music of Tagore and the mysticism of Yeats. He was the 'finest flower' in the renaissance of modern Punjab.

Bhai Vir Singh was very versatile. He was poet, novelist and critic. He found spiritual lessons in the objects of Nature. The *Kikar Tree* is a symbol of the spiritual seeker who must face the slings and arrows of worldly people. His poetry throbs with the longing of the individual sou to rejoin the Universal Soul. The hurdle between man and God is the Ego. Once that is subdued, man may meet God, face to face. He would find beauty and God's presence in the ordinary things of life. He believed mar could find peace and bliss through self control and spiritual effort.

Dr. Vir Singh was also a historical novelist. His important works it this genre are *Sundri, Bijay Singh* and *Satwant Kaur*. Their popularity, i: such that they have been reprinted many times.

Dr. Vir Singh sang of the struggles of the village folk. He wrote poem on freedom and patriotism. Bhai Vir Singh was not only a philosopher but also a stylist. Even his prose captures the dignity and harmony of poetry. *Kalgidhar Chamatkar* is full of purple passages. A registered society-*Bhai Vir Singh Sahitya Sadan*-is now busy publishing his works and popularising them among the masses. His centenary was celebrated in India and abroad in 1972.

90. What do you know of Sikh Paintings?

The Sikh school of painting is a distinct contribution to Indian art. The School originated in the days of Maharaja Ranjit Singh who was a liberal patron of arts. He also employed artists to decorate and panel the Golden Temple, Amritsar.

According to W.G. Archer, there are three distinct branches of the Sikh school: Guler Paintings, Kangra Paintings and Lahore Paintings. Guler became a part of Ranjit Singh's kingdom in 1813. Guler artists who had worked earlier on Rajput themes, now began to experiment with Sikh themes like the portraits of Sikh Gurus and Sikh dignitaries. The Kangra painters, when Kangra came under the control of Raja Sher Singh, son of Maharaja Ranjit Singh, portrayed Sikhs as aristocrats and lovers. The Lahore painters specialised in portraits of water colour miniatures. Schoefft, a Hungarian artist, drew sketches of the Golden Temple in the days of Raja Sher Singh. Between the fall of the Sikh empire and the twenties of this present century, flourished Sikh painters like Kishan Singh of Kapurthala, Bishan Singh of Amritsar and Kapur Singh.

Sikh painting is primarily of portraiture. It deals with historical characters and historical events. Sikh portraiture developed from the political struggle and it is through understanding the roles which certain individuals played, that we can understand their significance in painting.

One of the outstanding painters was Amrita Shergill (1913-41). Another artist named Gian Singh did a good deal of fresco painting on the inner walls and arches of the Golden Temple. His work in human, religious, floral and zoological motifs may be seen on the roof and corridors of the Temple. His technique is called *Mohra Qashi*.

Among contemporary painters, S.G. Thakur Singh and Sobha Singh are prominent. S. Kirpal Singh has executed a number of large canvas paintings for the S.G.P.C. He has dealt particularly with themes of the persecution of the Sikhs by the Mughal Governments in the 17th and 18th centuries. An exhibition of paintings of Guru Nanak was held in November, 1965, at Delhi by the "1969 Group." Mr. W.G. Archer has printed 119 plates in his book entitled *Paintings of the Sikhs* London (1966). The latest book entitled *Sikh Portraits by European Artists,* and ed. ed by F.S. Aijazuddin also throws light on the social and cultural leaders of the Punjab.

91. Give a brief history of the Golden Temple.

Guru Ramdas wanted to give the Sikhs a central place of worship. For this reason he founded a township, called after his name in 1577. In 1589, Guru Arjan requested a Muslim divine named Mian Mir, to lay the foundation of the Sikh Temple. This is known as *Har Mandar*— God's House—popularly called the Golden Temple. The temple is an example of religious emotion exemplified in marble, glass, colour and gold. The shrine is encircled by a beautiful artificial lake: "The pool of nectar— Amritsar." The reflections of the Temple building in the water strikingly magnify the artistic concept of the whole structure.

The other seat of Sikh Power called 'Akal Takht' was started in 1609 by Guru Hargobind for the holding of *Diwans* (Congregations) and other special celebrations. It was partly rebuilt after the army attack in June 1984.

The Muslim Governor of Lahore took possession of the temple in 1736. Bhai Mani Singh made an attempt to hold a special *Diwali Diwan* in the temple in 1768. This proved unsuccessful and cost him his life. Lakhpat Rai, the commandar of Mughal forces, occupied Amritsar in 1741.

Ahmed Shah Durrani attacked Amritsar on 10th April, 1762, damagd the temple and desecrated the tank. The Sikhs avenged this sacrilege by attacking the rear of his army.

The Golden Temple is regarded as an outstanding example of "Sikh architecture". It combines in its own right Hindu and Islamic features. Its styling adapts Moghul design with elaborations. Among its typical external features are four *chhattries* or kiosks which ornament the corners of Har Mandar's base. Inverted and guilded lotus flowers form its domes. Use is also made of oriel windows with shallow elliptic cornices supported on brackets. The arches are enriched with inlaid semiprecious stone foliations while the inner walls in addition to guilding and foliations also carry fresco paintings using the technique of *Mohra Qashi**

The present temple and its decorations were undertaken in the times of Maharaja Ranjit Singh. He donated many precious articles. The Golden Temple came under popular control in November 1920. The recent broadening of the *Parkarma* and the development of the Central Sikh Museum have added to the attractions of the temple. The desilting of the tank was last done in 1973. Special celebrations were held in the Golden Temple in October 1977 on th 400th Foundation Day of the city of Amritsar. The army attack on the Golden Temple in June 1984 has left scars on the super-structure.

92. Give an account of the Singh Sabha Movement.

The origin of the Singh Sabha Movement lay in the realisation by the Sikh leaders of the Eighteen seventies (last century) that Sikhism was dominated by Hindu practices and should be reformed to accord with the ideals of the Sikh Gurus. The movement was also reacting to the proselytizing activities of the Christian missionaries and the Hindu Arya Samaj movement in the Punjab.

The immediate cause of the beginning of the movement was the decision of four Sikh students of the Amritsar Mission School, early in 1873, to embrace Christianity. It gave a rude shock to the Sikh leaders. They succeeded in persuading these students to change their decisions and to continue living as Sikhs. A meeting of Sikh leaders, including prominent Gianis, Nirmalas and Udasis was held at Amritsar, on Ist October, 1873. As a result of their deliberations, a society named "Sri Guru Singh Sabha" was constituted and registered under existing law. The objectives of the Singh Sabha movment were to propagate the principles of Sikhism in its pure form, to remove untouchability, to perform Sikh ceremonies at the time of birth, marriage and death, to publish literature on the Sikh religion and history, to popularise the teaching of Gurmukhi, to reclaim apostates (patits) and to provide secondary and higher educaton to Sikhs and others.

As the movement gathered momentum branches were started in

---

*Mohra Qashi: is a special kind of decorative plaster.

Lahore and other major towns of the Punjab. Under the leadership of Bhai Gurmukh Singh, it got Punjabi and Gurmukhi recognised as subjects of study at the college level. It also started a Punjabi weekly in 1880 called "Gurmukhi Akhbar". Thereafter, Singh Sabhas sprang up all over India and reorganised Sikh missionary work in their areas by encouraging Ragi-groups and training preachers.

The Centenary of the Singh Sabha movement was celebrated in 1973 by the Singh Sabha Shatabdi Committee, in Amritsar. Now it has a permanent form and it called the Kendri Sri Guru Singh Sabha with a Head Office in Amritsar and Administrative Office in New Delhi. It has also opened a regional Office for the U.K. Sikhs in London. It has organised a number of Seminars on Sikh themes and conventions all over India. It has also produced a lot of literature in Punjabi, expounding the doctrines and practices of Sikhism. It issues a monthly magazine in Gurmukhi called *Singh Sabha Patrika*. Recently it exposed the hypocrisies, heresies and criminal and malicious, activities of the Nirankari sect. It has started a missionary school at Mehrauli which offers a three-year course in Sikhism including *Gurbani, Kirtan,* History, Philosophy and Comparative Religion.

93. What do you know of the Chief Khalsa Diwan?

As early as 1873 a movement was started in the Punjab for protecting the 'Rights of the Sikhs' and for maintaining the prestige and purity of the Sikh faith. It was originally part of the Singh Sabha Movement. It became necessary to have a central organisation to co-ordinate the activities of local Singh Sabhas. A big religious congregation was held on 30th October, 1902, at Amritsar, for this purpose. At this meeting the *"Chief Khalsa Diwan"* was formed. It was registered under the Societies Registration Act of 1869, on the 9th July, 1904. The founder of the Diwan-Sir Sunder Singh Majithia-gathered around him sincere and zealous workers like Bhai Vir Singh, S. Harbans Singh of Attari, S. Trilochan Singh and Principal Jodh Singh.

The aim of the Diwan was four-fold: (i) to promote the social, economic and moral uplift of the Sikhs, (ii) to propagate the message of Sikhism, (iii) to remove illiteracy, (iv) to protect the political rights of the Sikhs and ensure the redress of their grievances, by constitutional means. The constitution of the Diwan provides for a broad based representation of the four *Takhats*, the Singh Sabhas and the missionary associations.

The Diwan has had considerable success in the cultural and educational fields. The educational committee of the Diwan-started in January, 1908-has held annual sessions of the All-India Sikh educational Conference. The Diwan has a large number of educational institutions under its management. A high percentage of literacy among the Sikhs, is an off-shoot of the educational effort of the Diwan. It has redressed many Sikh grievances against the discrimination of Sikhs in government services.

The Chief Khalsa Diwan actively encouraged the production of Punjabi literature. The Sikh Tract Society was affiliated to the Diwan. It took a leading part in the movements for the carrying of the *Kirpan* and *Achhut Udhar*. It also runs the Central Khalsa Orphanage. Homeopathic Hospital, Khalsa Parcharak Vidyalaya and Khalsa Hospital, Tarn Taran. Examining its past record, the Diwan provides a useful service to the Panth.

94. What do you know of the Gurdwara Reform Movement?

Towards the end of the 19th century, the Sikhs felt a need to recapture the glory of the Sikh faith by following its traditions. The Singh Sabha Movement had earlier prepared the ground for a revival of the Sikhism. Many of the old and historical Gurdwaras were under the control of the *Mahants*—professional priests. They used the offerings and income for their personal use. The aim of the Gurdwaras Reform Movement—*Akali Lahar* was to liberate the Gurdwaras from the arbitrary control of *Mahants* and to bring them under popular control. The Government and other vested interests, were against this popular movement. So the Sikhs had to undergo lots of hardship and terrible suffering in order to improve the administration of their religious shrines.

This popular movement gathered momentum with the *Parchar* of the Akalis. Moreover, the democratic principles of the Sikh Religion, under the extravagance and immorality of the *Mahants*, the need for removal of untouchability and the utilisation of Gurdwara funds for educational and charitable purposes, were responsible for its mass-appeal.

Perhaps, the first incident which focussed public attention on the need to improve the Gurdwaras was the famous Rakabganj case in 1914. The Government had demolished a part of the Gurdwara wall for the purposes of road-making. The Sikhs had to start an agitation to oppose this; ultimately the Government had to yield to public opinion.

The establishment of the Sikh League in 1919 helped the Gurdwara Reform Movement. The Sikhs practised peaceful non-cooperation with the Government. They demanded popular control of the Golden Temple and the Khalsa College, Amritsar. The Government transferred the management of the Khalsa College to a Sikh Managing Committee. The Sikh conference held at Amritsar in 1920 appointed a Committee for the management of Sikh temples.

The tragedies of *Nankana Sahib* (1921) *Panja Sahib, Guru-ka-Bagh* and *Jaito* brought untold misery to the Sikhs. Ultimately the Punjab Government acceded to its demands and passed the Sikh Gurdwara Act on 6th July, 1925. Thus finally bringing Sikh temples under the control of elected representatives.

95. What do you know of the Shiromani Gurdwara Prabandhak Committee?

The Shiromani Gurdwara Prabandhak Committee popularly known as the SGPC—is a statutory body constituted under an Act of the Punjab Legislature passed on 9th July 1925. It is invested with certain duties regarding the administration of Gurdwaras, educational programmes and the propagation of the Sikh faith. Its *Dharam Parchar Committee* is specifically meant for the publication of literature on Sikhism. It has produced a number of books and tracts on Sikhism in English and modern Indian languages.

The SGPC controls the golden Temple, the *Langar* attached to it, Guru Ramdas Nivas and Guru Ramdas Hospital, Amritsar. It also manages the Khalsa College Bombay, Mata Gujri College. Fatehgarh Sahib, Bhupindra Khalsa High School, Moga, Shri Guru Ramdas Khalsa High School, Amritsar and Guru Nanak Girls Higher Secondary School, Amritsar. It runs the Shahid Sikh Missions at Aligarh, Burhanpur and Hapur. In addition, the SGPC employs teams of *Ragis* and missionaries for the propagation of the Sikh faith in the Punjab and U.P. It also looks after the interests of those Sikh farmers who have settled in Ganganagar (Rajasthan) and Terai (U.P.)

The SGPC awards divinity scholarships to students who win the top positions in competitive examinations held every year. It provides teams and aid for *Amrit Parchar*. It has recently established a Central Sikh Museum where heir-looms, old manuscripts and paintings are displayed. The Central Sikh Ithas Research Board is one of its main departments. It also maintains a research and reference library on Sikh history.

Recently, the SGPC lent its support to the movement for the formation of a Punjabi State on a linguistic basis. The Central Government agreed to the linguistic division of Punjab and the new Punjab State was thus formed in November 1966.

96. What is the contribution of the Sikhs to the struggle for India's independence?

The part played by the Sikhs in the overthrow of British rule was significant. Recently it has been established that the first and second Sikh Wars were fought to prevent the British aggression in the Punjab.

After the fall of the Punjab, the Sikhs felt a nostalgia for the glories and achievements of the Sikh rule of Ranjit Singh's times. As early as 1860, Baba Ram Singh, leader of the Kuka or Namdhari movement, raised the banner of revolt against the British regime. Ram Singh was deported to Rangoon where he died in 1885. More than 66 of his followers were blown away from the guns in 1872 without any trial, by Mr. Cowan—a British civil servant.

In January, 1909, Indian leaders held a public meeting in Caxton Hall, London, to celebrate the birth anniversary of Guru Gobind Singh. There it was proclaimed that Sikhs all over the world should start an agitation for the liberation of India. In response to this clarion call, the Sikhs who had settled in foreign countries decided to continue the freedom struggle. In 1913, more than 200 Indians, mostly Sikhs, founded the well-known *Ghadar Party* in California to liberate India from the British yoke, by force of arms. Baba Gurdit Singh chartered a Japanese ship called *Komagata Maru* in 1913 and sailed with about 300 Indian nationals to Vancouver. The passengers were not allowed to disembark on the west coast of Canada and were subjected to many hardships. After two months of suffering, the passengers were made to land at Calcutta. Their procession was fired upon and more than 21 Sikhs lost their lives. The remaining Sikhs were arrested and sent to the Punjab.

The Sikhs again bore the brunt of General O'Dyer's persecution. In the *Jallianwallah Bagh* massacre (1919), more than 400 Sikhs lost their lives. The Sikhs took a leading role in the Indian National Army raised by Subhash Chandra Bose in 1942 for the liberation of India. General Mohan Singh organised the Sikh population of Malaysia and took part in the expulsion of British forces in South-East Asia. The Sikhs also took an active part in 'Quit India' movement in 1942. It is therefore, correct to say that the contribution of the Sikhs to freedom struggle has been substantial and significant.

97. What do you know of Guru Gobind Singh Foundation, Chandigarh?

Guru Gobind Singh Foundation was set up in Chandigarh in 1965 in order to organise the 300th Birth-anniversary of Guru Gobind Singh and to implement suitable projects in memory of the Tenth Guru. The Punjab Government gave a seed-grant of Rupees 12 lakhs, and donations were collected from the public both for the celebrations in 1966-67 and the establishment of suitable useful institutions. At the initiative of the Foundation, the weapons of Guru Gobind Singh were received from U.K. in Delhi on 1st January 1966, and they were displayed at various places throughout India.

The 300th birthday of Guru Gobind singh which fell on 17th January 1967 was celebrated by Sikhs all over the world. Special functions were held in historical Gurdwaras and other places connected with the Tenth Guru. The G.G.S. Foundation published more than a dozen books on the life and work of Guru Gobind Singh in English and Punjabi. The main projects and achievements of the Foundation are as under:

(i) Guru Gobind Singh Bhawan, Chandigarh, constructed on a four-acre plot provides a library, a book-store, a multi-purpose air-conditioned hall and seminar rooms.

(ii) Guru Nanak College was established at Madras in 1969 from generous grants given by the Foundation.

(iii) Guru Nanak Public School, Chandigarh was established at a cost of Rupees 8 lakhs.

(iv) A writers' Home called "Vidyasar" at a cost of Rupees 4.5 lakhs was established at Paonta Sahib (Himachal Pradesh). It provides a library and guest house for scholars.

(v) The Foundation provided funds for the constuctions of an Operation Theatre in the Ghani Khan Nabi Khan Hospital at Machhiwara.

(vi) The Foundation took a leading part in the inaugaration of Guru Gobind Singh Marg (National Highway) in 1973 and provided funds for the construction of a number of pillars on the route called "Dashmesh Pillars".

The Foundation organises lectures and seminars on Sikhism from time to time. It hosted the All-India Sikh Educational conference in 1981.

98. What do you know of Guru Nanak Foundation, New Delhi?

Guru Nanak Foundation was set up in 1965 to organise the Quincentenary celebrations of the birthday of Guru Nanak scheduled for 1969, and to promote Guru Nanak's teachings. The Government of India gave a special grant to the Foundation for the establishment of Guru Nanak Institute of Comparative Religions and a department of musicology at Delhi. The Foundation has both Sikhs and non-Sikhs on its Governing Body, consisting of 51 members.

The Foundation's activities and achievements are listed below:

1. Promotion of Sikh studies through Gurmat College, Patiala, which is affiliated to Punjabi University, Patiala for the M.A. Degree in Religious Studies.

2. Preparation of L.P. Records of Guru Nanak's Hymns in classical ragas. So far eight records have been released.

3. Establishment of Guru Nanak Public Library for the benefit of scholars and the public.

4. Holding of seminars on Sikhism from time to time.

5. Financial support for scholars working at the Institute for the Ph. D. Degree of Punjab University. Junior and senior scholarships are given to research students.

6. Publication of over 20 books on Guru Nanak in English, Hindi and Punjabi.

7. Guru Nanak Memorial lectures: This is an annual feature and

distinguished scholars are invited for lectures which are published later by the Foundation.

8. Inter-school Gurbani competition and Inter-college essay competition.

9. Preparation of a pictorial history of the Sikhs.

10. Publication of a bi-annual journal called "Studies in Sikhism and comparative religion." Three volumes have been published so far.

11. Establishment of a Sikh reference Library for collecting manuscripts and rare data is under the consideration of the Foundation.

12. An international Conference on "Religion and Peace" was organised by the Foundation in its auditorium in February 1985.

99. What do you know of Pingalwara, Amritsar?

Pingalwara literally means a home for the crippled. However, this institution caters to the needs of the handicapped, the insane and the terminally sick. It is primarily a rescue-home for the poor, helpless and maimed.

The promoter of the Pingalwara is Bhagat Puran Singh, a selfless and dedicated Sikh. He was born in Lahore and used to do voluntary service at Gurdwara Dera Sahib. He would clean the streets of Lahore and cremate the unclaimed dead. He took care of the destitute and took the sick to the hospital for treatment.

After the partition of India in 1947, Bhagat Puran Singh set up a centre at Amritsar. First, he had a few tents to accommodate the poor and the sick. Soon he got a plot of land and constructed a three storyed building to house 250 patients. The unclaimed bodies of those who die in Pingalwara are taken to the local medical college for teaching anatomy. Pingalwara receives grants from the government, Shiromani Gurdwara Parbandhak Committe, Amritsar and similar charitable institutions. Sikhs, both in India and abroad, collect funds and send them to the Pingalwara. Bhagat Puran Singh is an institution in himself. He is an unassuming and dedicated Sikh, who reminds one of Bhai Kanhiya, a Sikh of the Tenth Guru. Puran Singh is a true Sikh in the old tradition and has won public esteem for his humanitarian work all over India. He is called by various epithets—'Mother Teresa of Punjab', 'the bearded saint of Amritsar', 'Bhai Kanhiya of the twentieth century.'

Recently Bhagat Puran Singh got a cash award of Rs. 20,000/- from the Punjab Government and he donated it to the Pingalwara. He is hopeful of carrying on his selfless work till the end of his life. At the age of eighty, he maintains a busy schedule of service till late in the night. He has no worry about funds for the institute. He similingly declares: "This is God's work, and I feel confident that He will look after it." This institute is a registered charity and will continue to function after Bhagat Puran Singh's passing away.

100. Give an account of the Sikh-residents abroad.

Early in the twentieth century, many Sikhs migrated to British Columbia (Canada) to improve their economic prospects. However, on account of racial trouble, they had to face severe hardships, most were engaged in lumbering and the timber trade. Some of them migrated to the south in California (U.S.A.). They initially worked as farm-labourers and were later allowed to buy land after a great struggle. Wherever they settled, they opened Gurdwaras for the benefit of visitors and new settlers, these also served as community-centres.

After the partition of India in 1947, many Sikhs migrated from West Pakistan and settled in different countries. Professional Sikhs like doctors, teachers and engineers settled in the big cities of Canada and U.S.A. Uprooted farmers from the West Punjab went to North California in large number and settled round Stockton and Yuba city. They also brought their relatives and friends from the Doaba region of the Punjab. Now they own big ranches and orchards in California.

In 1969, Sardar Harbhajan Singh Puri of Delhi migrated to Canada and was subsequently thrown out of the country, he then went to Los Angeles and started Yoga classes there. He was able to get a large number of American students interested in Yoga. By and by, he introduced them to a form of Sikhism. He called his movement 3HO (Healthy, Happy, Holy Organisation). It spread all over the U.S.A. and a number of Ashrams were established. Many of his American Sikhs became the Khalsa of Guru Gobind Singh with yogiji as their head. They set up their own communities in Ashrams and participated in the cultural and economic life of important cities. The Sikh Dharma Brotherhood and the Khalsa

Council of the Western Hemisphere were established to carry the message of the Gurus to peoples of the West. The number of American Sikhs is on the increase.

Originally Sikhs came to Great Britain to study. However, after 1947, Sikhs from the Punjab migrated in large numbers to the industrial centres like London, Birmingham and West Yorkshire to work as labourers and technicians in factories. Today the Sikhs have their largest concentrations in Ealing, Southall and Eastham in Greater London. They have now more than two hundred Gurdwaras in the U.K. and some of them being run by the Ramgarhia community and others. Sikh children born and educated here are torn between two cultures—the culture of their parents and the culture of England. There is a great need to educate them on their rich parental heritage and Sikh tradition. Seminars, group discussions and literature written in English are of great use to Sikh youth in understanding their religion and culture. During the last ten years, many Sikhs from Africa mostly from Kenya, Uganda and Tanzania have also settled in Britain and have taken up various jobs, and some have opened shops and ware-houses. The population of Sikhs today in U.K. is about a quarter million.

A third concentration of Sikhs abroad is in Malaysia and the Far East. There they work as doctors, lawyers, engineers, teachers, in the Police and the Army. They play an important role in the political, economic and social and cultural life of the cities in which they live. In Malaysia, they have Gurdwaras in Kualalumpur, Seramban, Perak, Penang, Kedah, Sarawak and other places. The Sikhs settled in Thailand, Singapore and Hong Kong also have *Gurdwaras* there. They donate liberally to local charitable institutions. The Singapore Sikhs have set up a Sikh Resource Centre at Gurdwara Katong. Apart from distributing Sikh literature, this centre recently helped in the publication of books on 'Sikh Studies' for the G.C.E. Cambridge Course. Two text-books have been issued by the Sikh Advisory Board and two more for teachers will be published soon. A one-week seminar for teachers of Sikh Studies was held in Singapore in September 1985. It is not possible to enumerate the achievements of the Sikhs in these various regions. The total number of Sikhs settled abroad is over one million. They are loyal to the countries in which they live but they look to the Punjab and its traditions, for spiritual inspiration.

V. Sacred Literature

101. What is Gurbani?

The sacred literature of Sikhism is called *Gurbani* which means the Guru's word—A song message—as enshrined in Guru Granth Sahib. In Sikhism, the Guru Means 'The *Word*' and not the physical body. God revealed the *bani* through the Guru and it will ultimately lead one to its source. The *bani* is the Guru and the Guru is the *bani*- One who expounds or explains the *bani* cannot have the status of a Guru. He is a mere teacher or missionary. Any compositions other than those of the Gurus and those approved by them are unacceptable to Sikhs.

Some people make much of the apparently contradictory statements in *Gurbani*. The hymns have been written to suit different stages in spiritual development. For example, in one hymn, Guru Nanak says that with individual effort, it is possible to realise God; in another hymn he says that austerities and meditation are of no avail without God's grace. With understanding and patience, it is possible to reconcile the so-called contradictions. In this instance, prayer in the beginning is due to personal effort, but later on, it can be seen that this effort was itself induced or assisted by God. Without His order—*Hukam*—it is impossible for man to do anything. Effort on its own only produces egoism and even frustration. Humility is essential for the winning of God's Grace.

The reading of *Gurbani* requires concentration, understanding and heart-searching. Lip-utterance on its own is of no avail. The devotee must meditate on the *message* of *Gurbani*. This alone can help him to rid his mind of evil thoughts and make it pure enough to receive the Name.* The true devotee drinks this nectar because it gives him inner satisfaction and inner peace. The percolation of Gurbani into the inner consciousness is as fruitful as the seasonal rain to a ploughed field. Guru Nanak says, "Make a boat of the sacred Name then, with the oars of faith, cross the ocean of illusion."

According to Sikhism, *Gurbani* is the panacea for all human ills and sin. It is for the individual to find out which hymn or *Salok* appeals to him

---

*The holy Spirit

and is related to his spiritual need. If he feels comforted by the hymns of the Guru, he should realise that meditation is his spiritual need.

102. What do you know of Sri Guru Granth Sahib?

Guru Arjan compiled the *Adi Granth* popularly known as the *Granth* which contains the hymns of the first five Gurus and some of the *Bhagats* of medieval India. He installed this scripture in the Har Mandar in 1604. This copy got into the hands of Dhirmal, the son of Guru Har Gobind. Subsequently some Sikhs forcibly obtained the copy from Dhirmal and presented it to Guru Tegh Bahadur. He returned it to Dhirmal. Guru Gobind Singh dictated the entire *Granth* to Bhai Mani Singh and incorporated the hymns of Guru Tegh Bahadur, in 1706 at Damdama Sahib. At the time of his death, Guru Gobind Singh conferred permanent Gurudom on the *Guru Granth Sahib* (1708).

The *Guru Granth Sahib* contains 5894 hymns. The largest number of hymns (2216) were contributed by Guru Arjan. The 937 hymns of fifteen *Bhagats* and eleven *Bhatts* whose compositions tallied with the gospel of Sikhism were also included. Here the Hindu, the Muslim the Brahmin and the untouchable, meet on an equal footing. From the linguistic point of view, it is a treasury of old "Hindi dialects."

Music forms the basis of the classification of the hymns. They follow a defnite metrical system. The total number of Ragas* is 31. Under each *Raga*, the hymns are arranged thus: *Chaupadas. Ashtapadas*, long poems, *Chhands, Vars*, and poems of *Bhagats*. The Guru Granth Sahib is written in the Gurmukhi script and contains 1430 pages.

Guru Arjan commenting on the nature of the *Granth* said: "In this dish are placed three things: Truth, Harmony and Wisdom. These are seasoned with the Name of God which is the basis of all; whoever eats it and relishes it, shall be saved." It is a work of divine inspiration. It is both metaphysical and ethical reality and imagination, mysticism and philosophy. According to Prof. Puran Singh, it is a scripture for all nations. It is a lyric of divine love, on which all the people of the earth subsist of such glowing lyrical power. The Guru Granth Sahib is of one Song, one Idea and one Life." Guru Arjan wanted the book to be translated into foreign languages

---

*Raga in Indian classical music means a pattern of melodic notes.

because it is the scripture of universal religion. It is a unique treasure, a noble heritage for all mankind.

103. What do you know of the Dasam Granth?

Guru Gobind Singh was not only an exceptional warrior but also a creative genius. His scholarship in Persian, Hindi and Punjabi enabled him to write verses in different poetic forms. He patronised fifty-two poets at his court. The most important of them were Bhai Nandlal Goya and Sainapat.

The Dasam Granth, compiled by Bhai Mani Singh after Guru Gobind Singh's death, contains more than 1400 pages in Brij Bhasha, Persian and Punjabi. The contents are mythological, philosophical and autobiographical. The two main themes of the Guru's work—authentically ascribed to him—are in praise of the Almighty and to the power of the sword. The verses were meant to stir the people in his times with patriotic and martial fervour. The following compositions are definitely written by the tenth Guru.

The *Jaap Sahib*: This is a unique composition in a variety of metres, praising the characteristics and power of God.

Bachitra Natak: A wonderful drama, an intimate autobiography recounting the mission of the Guru.

Akal Ustat, Shabad Hazare, Tatees, Swayya: These hymns enshrine the praises of the Timeless One in telling phrases and striking similes. Here is an example:

"As waves beating on the shingle,

Go back and in the ocean mingle,

So, from God come all things under the sun,

And to God return, when their race is run".

Zafar-Nama: This poetic epistle in Persian was addressed to the Emperor Aurangzeb and throws light on the Guru's opposition to tyranny and fanaticism.

What impresses one in the Dasam Granth is the excellence of the poetic technique and the choice of words and epithets. Guru Gobind Singh—even when the situation appeared desperate, after his leaving

Anandpur—never at all doubted victory or his unflinching faith in God.
"With Thee I will in adversity dwell but

Without Thee, a life of ease is a life in hell."

The versatility of this saint-soldier in composing devotional verses shows the richness of his mind, his spiritual attainment and heroic grandeur.

104. What is the literary value of the poetry of the Gurus?

Apart from its mysticism and spiritual depth, the poetry of the Gurus throws light on their contemporary situation. It lays bare the corruption and degradation of the society of their time and stresses the need of social reform and economic uplift. Guru Nanak and Guru Gobind Singh both recommended a just and humane administration, to the then rulers of India.

The hymns of the first five Gurus, the ninth and tenth Gurus, show an admirable use of the current figures of speech, apart from their metrical richness and sweetness. Imagery is used to simplify subtle thoughts and profound concepts. The images were taken from everyday life and common occurrence. The Gurus were keen lovers of nature and as such, have written glowing descriptions of panoramic beauty and the changes of season. Guru Nanak in *Barah Mah* (The Twelve Months), compares the monthly moods of nature to the inner conditions of man. The *Arti* is full of the wonders of the skyscape:

"In the salver of the sky,

The Sun and Moon are the lamps.

The luminous stars are the pearls." (A.G. p. 663)

Spiritual truths are conveyed through homely similes.

"Just as there is fragrance in the flower, and

Reflection in a mirror, so

Similarly God lives within us

Search for Him in your heart!" (A.G. p. 684)

"The sun is the same, the seasons are many, as

Many are the garbs of the Creator", sayeth Nanak (A.G. p. 12)

The Gurus used current proverbs and popular sayings to illustrate their fundamental ideas of spirituality:

"As is the dream of the night, so is this world."

"As is the staff in the hand of a blind person,

So is, to us, the Name of God."

There is, however, no deliberate attempt to refine or embellish the language. Sublimity and idealism have been presented with such simplicity that even unlettered people can understand their import. The hymns satisfy a longing for perfection and spiritual attainment. The poetry of the Gurus is valuable for both its sublime content and literary excellence.

105. Give the substance of the Japji.

The *Japji* contains the whole basis of the Sikh religion and philosophy. The theme—the evolution of spiritual life—is developed systematically.

As a first step, Guru Nanak defines God and sums up His attributes. The goal of human life is for a union with the Divine Being, often called salvation or *Nirvana*. This is achievable through self-surrender and a submission to God's *Hukam*. God is manifest in His creation. Nature obeys His law; like-wise we too, must obey Divine law.

How can a devotee merge with Divinity? Guru Nanak suggests that in the early hours of the morning the devotee should meditate on "His Name" and praise His Greatness. The disciple must follow the Guru's word.

The first step is to listen for the Name. By careful listening, the devotee becomes free from sorrow and sin. The second step is true and firm belief in "The Name." Those who have firm faith in "The Name" not only free themselves from the cycle of birth and death but also liberate others. Creation is in the play of God. Some people are busy in good works, while others are busy in crime and sin. Action is followed by reaction. As a man sows, so shall he reap.

The sovereign remedy is the remembrance of "God's Name"* Just as

*The invocation of the air of the "Holy Spirit".

dirty clothes are cleaned by soap, in the same way, man's evil is washed away by "The Name." God is vast and so is His universe. No Religious leaders can ever fathom His greatness. He has created millions of worlds and stars. No one can visualise His infinity. He alone knows Himself. He guides and controls the universe and all things are under His law. The conquest of one's Ego under the control of the 'self,' is the only way to merge the individual soul into the Universal soul.

There are five stages of spiritual life: *Dharm Khand, Gian Khand, Saram Khand, Karam Khand* and *Sach Khand.* To progress through these the disciple has to follow a strict discipline, namely to control the mind and body, fearlessness, steady perseverence and a constant remembrance of "The Name", in order to reach the goal. True devotees have radiant faces, beaming with Divine Light and they bring peace and happiness to countless other people—all who come in contact with them.

106. Give the substance of the Asa-di-var.

. Guru Nanak's *Asa-di-var* or the morning prayer, consists of *Slokas* and 24 *Pauris.* Guru Ramdas added 24 *Chhands* (Quatrains). A *var* or ode is a heroic measure, popular in the Punjab. This particular *var* is sung in the early morning in all Sikh Temples. Here Guru Nanak sings of the glory of God and "The Name". He details the process by which an ordinary man can become a perfect servant of God. Even so God's grace is essential, and one has to deserve it;

"God Himself shapes men as vessels, and brings them to perfection. In some is put the milk of loving kindness, others ever are set on the fire of passion. Some lie down to sleep on cushions, others stand to watch over them. God regenerates those on whom He looks with grace. (24)"

The hurdles on the path to divinity like the Ego, hypocrisy, evil thoughts and actions, are discussed and various remedies are suggested.

According to Prof. Teja Singh, the "Asa-di-var" resembles an ancient choral ode in Greek. There is a great similarity in the way both *var* and Ode are sung." It may be noted that there are 22 vars in the *Granth,* out of which three—including *Asa-di-var*—are by Guru Nanak. Often *Shabads** are

---

*Hymns

interspersed between *Pauris* and this provides for both a variation of musical score and changes of thought.

Krishna Chaitanya, an Indian musicologist writes about the effect of the chant of *Asa-di-var* as under:

"In musical impact it is like the plain chant of European Christianity. It is recitative which has taken wings, rather than an abstract arabesque of sound. In its musical texture, it is wholly different from plain chant. This is because plain chant, comes early in the evolution of European music, whereas the melodic pattern of the Asa-di-var is derived by the simplification, of a mature classical tradition."

We understand the message and feel the melody at the same time. When the *Asa-di-var* is sung before dawn—*Amrit Vela*—it produces a feeling of inner repose and peace.

Gramophone records of the *Asa-di-var* are available in the market. The most popular is that of the late Surjan Singh

107. Give the substance of Anand Sahib.

The Anand Sahib—or "The Song of Bliss"—is the spiritual and musical masterpiece of Guru Amardas. Some biographers have tried to make it a historical piece by stating that it was composed in 1554, after the birth of his grand-son called Sidh-yogi, to whom he gave the new name of Anand. This story is improbable, because the composition contains no reference to any event or the birth of any child. Its theme is of man's spiritual goal, namely the merger into the Divine Essence.

There is a development of thought in the Anand. The first stanzas state clearly that bliss can be obtained through the Guru. The Guru stands for the Revelation, the Shabad, or those utterances which include his teaching on the stages of the spiritual path. Are there no short cuts to the attainment of bliss? The Guru mentions the hurdles that stand in the way of the disciple. These are: human cleverness, family attachment, taboos, rituals, conformity to tradition and convention, the opportunism of leadership and the compromise with principles. Stanzas six to twenty all deal with these obstructions.

What then are sources of bliss? These are the true submission to the commands of the Guru, the performance of acts of charity and selfless service, the association with holy people and the rememberance of the Holy Name. Stanzas twenty-one to twenty five tell us about the God-oriented person—the Sunmukh—who is radically different from the egoistic worldly person—the Bemukh. The disciple follows in the foot-steps of the Guru and sings of the Lord's praise in the company of saints or holy congregration.

Stanzas twenty-six to thirty four deal with the temptations of *Maya*, these grip man right from his birth. Attachment to his near and dear ones, immersion in the satisfaction of his desires and in meeting the demands of his relatives. How his thirst for such mundane things remains un-quenched. The more he gets, the more he wants.

Stanzas thirty five to thirty nine deal specifically with the functions of the human body and its sense-organs. A body becomes blessed if it is devoted to God. That fulfils the purpose of man's coming into the world. The eyes are blessed if they see the Lord pervading the whole universe. The ears are meant to hear the Truth and the song of God's glory. If man dedicates his senses to the attainment of spiritual goals, God opens to him, the door to His treasures. He can then sing the "Song of Bliss" in the home of his own soul. He who remembers God is loved by Him. The last stanza, number forty, enumerates the benefits of *Anand*. It banishes all tension and sorrow. Those who sing it or listen to it with devotion, become purified and liberated. the Unstruck Music of the Cosmic Melody is then recognised by them with great joy. Such noble souls may ultimately merge with the Lord.

The *Anand* has to be sung in the *Ramkali Raga* to make its full impact on the mind. The intellectual appreciation of these philosophical concepts is intensified by an aesthetic delight in its musical rendering. As the five kinds of musical hymns—Panch Shabad—mentioned, echo in one's memory, the vital truths and higher values of the *Anand* transport one to the mental realms of beauty and bliss.

108. Give the substance of the Sukhmani Sahib?

The *Sukhmani Sahib* is the simplest and most popular of all the Banis in the Guru Granth Sahib. Literally, "Sukhmani" means some thing which gives peace of mind or the touchstones for happiness. Guru Arjan's aim in writing the *Sukhmani*—The Psalm of Peace—was that the reader may feel composure of mind and a sense of inner bliss. Any person who is fed up with life or depressed by anxiety or otherwise afflicted will derive real consolation from it.

There is a gradual development of thought in the twenty-four cantos of the *Sukhmani*. In the first three cantos, Guru Arjan mentions the advantages of the practice of *"Nam,"* the remembrance of "the Name" *Simran* is the linking up with the divine, in a spirit of surrender, devotion and love. "The Name" helps in the normal business of life, and paves the way to spiritual progress. In cantos four to eleven, Guru Arjan gives his views on the God-man. Man's potentialities can be strengthened by divine grace. Man gets a vision of God through the company of holy men. The God-man is not the *vaishnavite*, or the salvationist or the touch-nothing mystic. He is one who fulfills the duties of a normal life: "The God-enlightened man lives like the lotus, pure amidst the impurities of the world." All the seekers, at one stage or another, seek God's help and turn to Him for strength and guidance. Cantos twelve to twenty mention the process by which God's grace can be merited. Self-conceit and the slander of saints bring their own punishment. Only by self-surrender, can one earn God's favour. God is "The Truth" and the Guru guides the lives of the disciples in righteous living. The Guru also inspires the devotees with a love of "The Name."

The last four cantos contain Guru Arjan's exposition of "The Name." The name covers both the personal and impersonal aspect of God. God transcends and unifies all creation. The singing to "The Name" gives man spiritual solace and inner peace. In the end, the Guru enumerates the rewards which the reading of the *Sukhmani Sahib* may bring to the reader. They are beauty, humility, wisdom, equanimity and God-realisation.

The Sukhmani Sahib is also regarded as the second expansion of "The Mul Mantra," the frist expansion being Japji Sahib and the third the entire Guru Granth Sahib.

VI. Worship, Ceremonies and the Future

109. What is the Naming Ceremony among the Sikhs?

Sikh ceremonies are not rituals or occasions for the display of affluence and ego, but acts of thanks-giving and prayer, suited to the occasion. There is no ceremony at the time of the birth of the child in a Sikh family, even though the event produces a feeling of joy among the near relatives. However, when the mother and child are in a position to move about, say a few weeks after the birth, the family takes the opportunity of performing the Naming Ceremony.

Generally a date is fixed by the parents, and the relatives and friends are informed of the date, time and venue. Generally the ceremony takes place in a Sikh Temple (Gurdwara). The family prepares some *Karah Prasad* at home or requests the Gurdwara to arrange for its preparation. The mother and child are taken to the Gurdwara. The family also takes a *Rumala* which is a piece of quality cotton or silk cloth about one metre square as a gift for the *Guru Granth Sahib* and sometimes sweets for distribution among the congregation. The *Granthi* or a senior member of the congregation present places a bowl of water near the Scripture. He places sugar-balls or pellets in the water and stirs the contents with a *Kirpan* (Sword) while reciting the first five *Pauries* of Guru Nanak's *Japji*. Sometimes some hymns are then sung to seek a blessing for the new-born. Then the general prayer, the *Ardas* (Supplication) is recited requesting good health and a long life for the child. After the Ardas a hymn is sung on behalf of the mother for the gift of meditation and *Gur-Sikhi*, for her child as under:

"O Son, this blessing is sought by your mother:

May you never forget the Lord of the universe even for a moment;

May the True Guru be kind to you and

May you come to a love for the society of the saints". (p. 496)

Thereafter a *Hukam* (a random reading from the Guru Granth Sahib) is made. The first letter of the first word of the reading becomes the initial letter of the child's name. For example if the first letter of the reading is "S", the child may be named Surjit Singh or Surinder Singh or any other name beginning with the letter "S". If the newborn is a girl, her name would likewise begin with "S" but will end with "Kaur" in place of "Singh" There-after a few drops of *"Amrit"* or sweetened water prepared earlier, are put in the baby's mouth, while the remaining water is drunk by the mother. The ceremony ends with the distribution of *Karah-Pursad* and the placing of the *Rumala* on *Guru Granth Sahib*. Sometimes, *Langar* is also served to those present, though this is not compulsory.

In places where there is no Sikh Temple or where the child and the mother are not in a position to move out, the Naming Ceremony may be held in the home. Friends and relatives may be invited. One of those present will recite a hymn or two, prepare the *Amrit* as mentioned above and offer *Ardas* before one of the other Sikh scripture if the Guru Granth Sahib is not available. they may then take a *Hukam* from the *Pothi* or *Gutka*. (Selections of Gurbani or Hymns). They will then propose a name according to the first letter of the hymn read. Those present generally give the approval to a name by a *jaikara* or it may be left to the parents to choose a name later, but using the key initial letter from the *Hukam*. The use of caste names like Grewal, Arora etc. before or after the personal name is discouraged in the Sikh religion.

110. What is the Sikh baptism—Amrit?

Baptism is necessary before joining the Khalsa Panth. Guru Gobind Singh initiated the practice with the establishment of the order of the Khalsa in 1699.

The *Amrit* ceremony (baptism) is held in the presence of the *Guru Granth Sahib*. Five baptised Sikhs known for their piety are called *Panj Piyaras*, all wearing the five symbols—*Kesh* (long hair) *Kangha* (Comb), *Kachha* (Knickers), *Kara* (Iron wristband) and *Kirpan* (Sword) sit in front of the *Guru Granth Sahib*. One of the five explains the principles of Sikhism to those who want to be baptised. After the candidates have signified their acceptance, one of the five offers *Ardas*. Then all the five sit round an iron-vessel containing fresh water and a quantity of sweets—*Patasas*. They recite the five *Banis:* the *Japji*, *Jap*, ten *Swayyas*, *Chaupai* and *Anand Sahib*. The reciter stirs the water with a double-edged sword, a *Khanda*, which he holds in his right hand. After recitation is over, the five initiators stand up, holding the vessel in their hands. Each one of them then offers prayer (one of the five Banis) for the nectar just prepared.

As Each candidate receives five handfuls of *Amrit* (holy water) which he drinks shouting *Wahguruji ka Khalsa Wahguruji ki Fateh*. The Amrit is put five times in his eyes and five times on his hair while he repeats the above greeting. The *Amrit* that remains is sipped by all candidates to remove caste prejudice. The five initiators repeat the *Mul Mantra* five times, this is then repeated by the candidates. Then one of the five explains the vows of Sikh discipline—*Rahat*. The candidates are to regard themselves as sons of Guru Gobind Singh and Mata Sahib Kaur. Their home is Anandpur Sahib. They are to abstain from the four misdeeds: removing hair, eating *halal* meat, adultery and using tabacco. One of the five *Panj Piyaras* then offers *Ardas* and reads a passage from the Guru Granth Sahib. Those who adopt Sikhism for the first time receive a new name, ending in *Singh* for a male and *Kaur* for a female. All the baptised Sikhs then eat *Karah Parsad* from the same vessel. If a Sikh has done any of the four misdeeds—*Kurahats*—mentioned above, he has to be rebaptised after due confession and penance.

111. What is Anand Marriage?

The Anand form of marriage was given a statutory recognition in 1909, under the Anand Marriage Act. It has been observed since the early days of Sikhism. Sikh boys and girls are married according to its form when they are grown-up and fit to undertake matrimonial responsibilities. Marriages are generally arranged and assisted by parents, though there is no bar to the boy and the girl arranging it on their own.

The marriage ceremony is simple but impressive. The bride and the bridegroom along with their relatives and friends form a congregation in the presence of the *Guru Granth Sahib*. The couple and their parents then stand and an *Ardas* is offered to seek God's blessing. The person in charge of the function addresses the bride and the bridegroom individually and explains to them their duties in the new life which they are about to enter. Anand marriage is sacrament. The Guru is a witness to the marriage. No writing or document is necessary. The bridegroom is to vow fidelity to the wife—*Istribrat Dharam* while the bride is to vow fidelity to her husband—*Patibrat Dharam*. The husband is to protect the life and honour of his wife, she is to remain content with the lot of her husband and her treatment in the husband's house. The couple signify their consent by bowing before the *Guru Granth Sahib*. Then the scarf of the bridegroom is placed in the hands of bride. The *Granthi* or the officiating person, reads the *lavan*—the epithalamium of Guru Ramdas. Each stanza explains in detail a stage in the development of a life of love. The first stage is the performance of duties to the family and the community. The second stage is that of selfless love and holy fear which provide opportunities for devoted service and sacrifice—the discipline needed to facilitate the feeling of yearning and enthusiasm. Even troubles provide opportunities for service and sacrifice, and are therefore helpful to love. The third stage is that of detachment: *Vairag*. Human love is superseded by divine love. The fourth stage is that of harmony or union. The bride and bridegroom are completely identified with each other.

After the reading of each stanza, the couple go round the *Guru Granth Sahib*, the bridegroom leading the bride, while the stanza is sung to the accompaniment of musical instruments. After the completion of the *lavan*, the *Anand Sahib* is read. Finally the *Ardas* after which *Karah Parsad* is distributed to all present. Monogamy is practised by the Sikhs.

112. What is the Death Ceremony among the Sikhs?

On the death of a Sikh, his relatives and friends are informed, so that they may join the funeral ceremony on whatever day and date is fixed for the cremation. In foreign countries, a date and time is given by the crematorium authorities. As soon as the people gather for the funeral, the dead body is bathed then dressed in clean clothes with the five symbols of the Khalsa, and placed on a wooden frame or palanquin. The people form a procession and sing hymns as they carry the body to the cremation ground. In the west they form a motorcade and drive to the crematorium. No wailing or beating of the chest or breasts is allowed, for death is the natural end for every person. After the body reaches the cremation-place, the *Kirtan Sohila* is recited, for it is of special significance at this time. The Guru says:

This same call goes to all homes every day;

So remember that Lord who calls, O Nanak;

The day draws ever nearer for each one of us. (p. 12)

Then the *Ardas* (General Prayer) is recited, this seeks a blessing for the departed person. Then the nearest relation to the deceased lights the funeral pyre, electricity or gas, whichever is used for the cremation. When the ashes are collected they should be disposed of by throwing them into running water or the sea. No memorials or monuments may be erected at the place where the last remains of the deceased were disposed of.

After the cremation, the relatives and friends return to the house of the deceased, there they bathe and generally start a *Sadharan Path* for the benefit of the dead and his family. This complete reading of the Scripture is done by the relations and friends of the family; sometimes *pathis* are engaged in case of need. Generally, both in the morning and in the evening, *Kirtan* and *Katha* are performed. The passing away of a Sikh is no cause of grief or sorrow, for one submits to the Will of God. Those who have led pure lives are not in any way afraid of death. Kabir says in this connection:

Death of which men are afraid, gives me nothing but joy!

It is through the gate of Death that one may unite with the Lord of Bliss. (p. 1365).

The *path* (reading) of the Holy Scripture should be completed within nine days. On the tenth day, the relatives and friends of the family gather for the "Bhog" ceremony, at which the singing of hymns, and the last five pages of *Sri Guru Granth Sahib* are read. After the *Bhog*, Ramkali Sadd* is recited for the benefit of the family of the deceased. The Gurus emphasised the rememberance of God's name as the means of consolation for the bereaved family. After *Ardas* and a *Hukam*, *Karah-Prasad* is distributed among those present. Sometimes Langar (Free food) is also served, though it is not compulsory. Presents are then sometimes destributed to the grand children and donations are announced for charities or religious organisations.

Sometimes another small ceremony is held to mark the occasion. This is called. *Dastar-bandi* (turban tying). The eldest member of the family is declared as the new Head of the family and given a turban ceremoniously. This is a token of his new responsibility for looking after the family and estate of the departed person. He is now regarded as the new chief of the family, responsible for the care of the children and other dependents of the family.

---

* Ramkali Sadd: This composition which is based on call of death is on page 923 of Guru Granth Sahib.

113. Describe the Sikh Temple.

Guru Nanak started the first Sikh assembly at Kartarpur in 1521. This was the beginning of a religious congregation called Dharmsala (place or seat of religion). In the mornings and the evenings the followers of Guru Nanak formed a *Sangat* (congregation) and hymns were sung by the Guru and Mardana often in chorus with all present. Later on, such sessions were held in the homes of the Guru's followers. The second Guru—Guru Angad—added another activity to the routine of work by teaching Punjabi in the Gurmukhi script. This was called the *Pathshala*. Here children gathered, to learn the script of the Guru's hymns. Guru Amardas. The Third Guru extended the Free Kitchen. The Fourth Guru established an ideal centre for work at Amritsar, while the Fifth Guru built the *Harmandar Sahib* later (called the Golden Temple.) Almost all the Gurus set up temples wherever they went or whenever they acquired a group of followers. These temples were called Gurdwaras which mean the door (home) of the Guru.

A Sikh temple today is not only a place of worship, but also a community-centre. A Free Kitchen (langar) is always a part of a temple. The Gurdwara is also used for performing the birth, marriage and death ceremonies of Sikhs. The Scripture is called *Sri Guru Granth Sahib*. It contains the musical compositions of the first five Gurus, the Ninth Guru and medieval-India saints—*Bhagats*—both Hindu and Muslim. It is kept in a central place on a raised platform and under a canopy. A man sits behind holding a *Chauri* (made from feathers or hair), which he waves from time to time in token of respect for "The Word" of the Guru. The worshippers sit on a carpet, men on one side and women on the other. They listen to the musicians or the lecturer. The most important Sikh Temples of Doctrinal Authority are the *Akal Takhat* Amritsar, *Kesgarh Sahib* at Anandpur, *Patna Sahib, Hazur Sahib*, at Nander and *Damdama Sahib*.

Sikh festivals like Diwali, Baikashi and *Gurpurbs* are celebrated in all Gurdwaras. Then the sessions are long and well attended. Special lectures are arranged to explain to the audience the significance of each occasion or historical event. Apart from the kitchen and dining hall, there are rooms set apart for the accommodation of travellers and visitors. Some big temples have a library and reading room, a Sikh Museum and school. Welfare projects like widow-homes, orphanges, dispensaries or clinics are run by many historical Gurdwaras in India. A Gurdwara is managed by a committee elected from the congregation, according to its registered Constitution. These elections are being held annually.

The Historical temples in India follow a certain design of architecture called Indo-Sarsenic. Temples in foreign countries may be housed in any building. Some of the Grudwaras in U.K. have purchased former Christian churches and then altered them to suit their needs. Usually there is a tall flag-pole—*Nishan Sahib*—covered with cloth and with a yellow flag bearing the Sikh Insignia. A Sikh temple is open to all people—whoever they may be.

114. Describe the Sikh Worship.

Generally a Sikh Temple—Gurdwara—remains open throughout the day, so that worshippers can offer prayers at any time convenient to them. However, in India, two services are held daily in every Sikh temple, one in the morning and the other in the evening. In the morning *Asa-di-Var* is sung or recited, this is followed by the Anand Sahib, the *Ardas* (supplication) and a *Hukam* (a random reading of a hymn of the Scripture), then follows the distribution of *Karah Prasad* (consecrated cooked food. Made of flour, clarified butter and sugar). In the evening, *Rehras* and *Chaupai* are recited by the *Granthi* (reader of the Scripture) or by the *sangat* (congregation). Then some hymns are sung by the *ragis* (musicians) or recited by the *sangat*. After an *Ardas* and a *Hukam Karah Prasad* is then distributed finally, the Guru Granth Sahib is ceremoniously wrapped up and taken to its special place for the night.

On festivals like *Gurpurbs* (Guru's festivals) days commemorating the birth, accession, death anniversary or other special occasions and *Akhand Path* (continuous reading of the Scripture for about 48 hours by the relays of readers) is held and the *Ardas* is offered. This is followed by programme of *Kirtan* (hymnal singing) and Katha (discourse). On such occasions the free kitchen—*Langar*—is open throughout the day.

Sikhs generally bathe in mornings before going to the Gurdwara. They take off their shoes at the gate then wash their hands and feet if suitable arrangements exist. When they enter the main hall, they kneel down and bow before the Guru Granth Sahib, they also make an offering in cash or kind. Any non-Sikhs must cover their heads with a cap or a handkerchief. They are not allowed to take any form of tobacco, alcohol or narcotics inside the temple.

The congregation sits crosslegged on the floor/carpet, the use of chairs is not permitted. In some cases, old and infirm people are allowed cushions for their comfort. There is no priesthood in Sikhism, but for the benefit of the congregation, a *Granthi* or *Sewadar* (care-taker) may be employed to read the Scripture; perform ceremonies or help in the *Langar*. Often professional musicians called Ragis sing hymns from the Scripture in the prescribed ragas (melody-patterns) and *talas* (rhythms), accompanied by a harmonium and *tabla* (pair of drums). In the absence of any musicians, the congregation sings the hymns in chorus.

115. What is the place of sacred music—Kirtan—in Sikhism?

Sacred music, *Kirtan*, means "singing the praises of God." It is devotional music. Generally in the Gurdwara, musicians either sing alone or request the *Sangat* to repeat after them the lines of the hymn in chorus. This is congregational hymn-singing and has a soothing effect on the mind. The Sikh sacred music—*Gurmat Sangeet*—falls into two categories; classical music and folk music. Classical music pruned of ornamentation becomes devotional music. Folk music includes those *vars* in the ballad form which enshrine the praise of God.

The Sikh Gurus themselves composed hymns to be sung according to certain musical scores. The scores were suited to the spirit and the content of the hymn. The best way to sing a hymn is to do so in its own *raga* and according to its own musical notation. The Sikh Gurus harmonised the contents of poetry with the characteristics of the raga. 31 different ragas have been used in the *Guru Granth Sahib*.

Guru Nanak encouraged his followers to practise hymn-singing at dawn, because at that period of the day, all is quiet and the mind is receptive to the soft strains of music and the surrounding atmosphere of stillness. This helps in the absorption of the healing power of *Nam*. According to the Gurus, *Kitran* is food for the soul. It is a permanent treasure which can never be depleted. Whoever performs *Kirtan* or listens to it, comes nearer to God. Their troubles and miseries lessen and their minds gain peace and equipoise.

Guru Nanak encouraged his companion—Mardana—to do *Kirtan* at all times. Guru Amardas wanted the *Sangat* to join in group-singing. Though there are professional singers, the best Kirtan is one in which the entire *Sangat* sings in chorus, then all can partake of this divine food as every one needs it. Sikhs pray for the strength to sing God's praises.

For Sikhs the slow and deep strains of their devotional music please the soul like the gentle drops of rain, please the dried out earth. The soul drinks the musical nectar and immerses itself in the divine Name. The devotional music in India would never have reached its present height, but for the impact of the hymns of the *Guru Granth Sahib.*

116. Is there any organised priesthood in Sikhism?

Guru Amardas organised the propagation of the Sikh faith. He divided the country into 22 dioceses—*Manjis* each in the charge of a devout Sikh. Daily *Kirtan* was held by all congregations (*Sangats*). The Guru himself trained many travelling missionaries, including women, they were moved into different parts of India to spread Sikhism.

These missionaries, then called '*massands*' collected offerings from the Sikhs for the Guru, and sometimes misappropriated them for their personal use. In due course, they became powerful as a separate group and started harassing the poor and innocent Sikhs. They moved about like *Jagirdars* and *Zamindars*, with pomp and pageantry, and accompanied by their servants and retainers.

Guru Gobind Singh received several complaints regarding the misdeeds of these '*massands*' from sikhs living in different parts of India. He looked into the complaints made against each one. The guilty were duly punished and the order of *massands* was abolished.

Since that time there has been no professional priesthood, in any form, among the Sikhs. The idea of clericalism as opposed to secularism, of a different morality for the churchman and for the layman has no place in Sikhism. There are neither hereditary priest nor monks. Sikhism does not prescribe a particular dress or uniform for a saint. It does not enforce the vow of celibacy. In its temples, any one can perform the services for *Kirtan* and *Katha*. The person known as a '*Granthi*' is merely a reader of Guru Granth Sahib. He is a *Pathi. Kirtan*-groups generally consist of amateurs. Even those who are professionally-trained as singers cannot be priests, because there is no such office or designation.

Women are allowed to take part in *Kirtan* and *Katha* on equal terms with the men. They may lead and participate in all ceremonials like baptism, marriage and funeral, where readings from the Guru Granth Sahib are common to all such functions.

It is not generally understood that all Sikhs are under a sacred duty to try to impart a knowledge of their religion (SIKHISM) to the rest of the world.

117. Mention the important Sikh festivals.

Sikh festivals are many, for example general festivals like the birthdays, the accession anniversaries of the Gurus, the death anniversaries of the Gurus, in addition to other special events. There are also local festivals like *Maghi* (celebrated at Mukatsar in Punjab) *Holla Mahalla* (celebrated at Anandpur and Fatehgarh Sahib). However, these are five big festivals which are celebrated by the Sikhs all over the world. These festivals are not meant for solely entertainment, pleasure of food and frolic, but are occasions for the revitalisation of faith and rededication to the principles and practices of Sikhism. These celebrations are open to all men and women without distinction of caste, creed or colour and take form in devotion and worship, through *Kirtan* (hymnal singing), *Katha* (discourse or lecture) and *Ardas* (supplication), *Karah Parsad* (consecrated food) and *Langar* (free food in the community kitchen).

(i) *Guru Nanak's Birthday:* Guru Nanak is the Founder of Sikh religion. He was born on 20th October 1469 at Talwandi, now in Pakistan. The actual birthday-anniversary varies, according to the dates of the Bikrami Sambat. The celebrations generally last for three days, though in some small villages or Gurdwaras, there is only a one-day celebration on the actual birthday. Two days before the birthday, an *Akhand Path* (continuous reading of Sri Guru Granth Sahib which takes about 48 hours, by relays of readers called *pathis*) is held in the Gurdwara (Sikh Temple). One day before the birthday, a procession is organised through the town, led by *Panj Piyaras* (Five Khalsas) and the *Palki* (palanquin) of *Sri Guru Granth Sahib* followed by teams of singers, singing hymns, brass-band playing different tunes and groups of devotees singing in chorus. On the actual Birthday a *Diwan* (religious session) begins early in the morning at about four O'clock, with the singing of the *Asa-di-var* (morning prayer) followed by the hymns from the Scripture. Then follows the *Bhog* (reading of last five pages) of the *Akhand Path* after which more, *Kirtan* and *Katha*, lectures and the recitation of poems in praise of the Guru. This celebration goes on till lunch-time, when *Langar* is served to all.

Some Guardwaras also hold night-services. These begin soon after sunset when the *Rehras* and *Chaupai* are recited. Then follows *Kirtan* till late in the night. Sometimes a *Kavidarbar* (poetic symposium) is held, to enable poets to pay their tributes to the Guru in their own words. At about 1.20 A.M. (the actual time of the birth of Guru Nanak) the congregation sings the praises of the Guru and recites the Holy Word. The function ends at about 2 A.M.

(ii) *Guru Gobind Singh's Birthday:* Guru Gobind Singh is the tenth Guru of the Sikhs. He was born at Patna on 22nd December 1666. The celebrations are similar to those for the three-day schedule of Guru Nanak's Birthday. Those Sikhs who cannot join the main celebrations for some reason or live in places where there is no Sikh Temple, hold a celebration in their own homes and themselves perform *Kirtan*, *Ardas* and distribute *Karah Parsad*.

(iii) *The Installation of Sri Guru Granth Sahib as permanent Guru.*

Three days before passing away, Guru Gobind Singh conferred perpetual Gurudom on *Sri Guru Granth Sahib* on 3rd October 1708. The Sikh Scripture is also called the Eleventh Guru. On this day a special one-day celebration is held with *Kirtan*, *Katha*, lectures, *Karah-Parsad* and *Langar*. Sikhs then rededicate themselves to follow the teachings contained in the Guru Granth Sahib. In all Sikh temples, the Guru Granth Sahib presides and holds the most prominent place. In some Gurdwaras, an *Akhand Path* is read as a part of the celebration.

(iv) *Baisakhi:* This is the Birthday of the Khalsa (the pure ones). Guru Gobind Singh started the Khalsa brotherhood with his 'baptism of steel' on 30th March 1699. This one-day celebration is held in Gurdwaras with *Kirtan*, *Katha*, lecture and *Karah-Parsad*, *Ardas* and *langar*. In addition, the Amrit ceremony is held and Amrit is given to those who offer themselves for baptism. Sikhs after taking Amrit, are called Khalsa. In some Gurdwaras, an Akhand Path is read as a part of the celebration.

(v) *Diwali:* The Sikhs celebrate Diwali—generally regarded as a Hindu festival—because Guru Hargobind came back to Amritsar on this day in 1620, after his release from Gwalior jail. The one-day celebration is held with *Kirtan, Katha,* lectures, *Karah-Parsad, Ardas* and *langar* in the Gurdwara. Diwali means festival of lights. So in the evening, illuminations are lit and fire-work displays are held, both in Gurdwaras and in the homes of Sikhs to express their joy at the return of the Sikhs' Guru to *Sri Akal Takht* (the Throne of the Timeless one) at Amritsar.

In addition to the above festivals, celebrations are held in memory of the martyrdom anniversary of Guru Arjan in summer season, and the martyrdom anniversary of Guru Tegh Bahadur in winter, in every Sikh temple.

118. What are the Seats of Authority (Takhats) in Sikhism?

'Takhat' which literally means a throne or seat of authority is a result of historical growth of Sikhism. There are five Takhats. The first and the most important one was established by Guru Hargobind in 1609. It is called "Akal Takhat" (the Throne of the Timeless God) and is situated just opposite the gate of Harmandar Sahib—the Golden Temple, Amritsar. The Guru established it, because he thought that secular and political matters should not be considered in the Golden Temple, which is meant purely for worship of God. Here the Guru held his court and decided matters of military strategy and political policy. Later on, the Sikh Commonwealth (Sarbat Khalsa) took decisions here on matters of peace and war and settled disputes between the various Sikh groups. The *Sarangi* singers sung the ballads of the Sikh Gurus and warriors at this place and robes of honour (saropas) were awarded to persons who rendered distinguished services of the community of men in general.

The second seat of authority is called "Takhat Sri Patna Sahib". Guru Tegh Bahadur lived with his family here in 1665. Here was born Guru Gobind Singh. The building which was partly damaged by the great earthquake of 1934 has been rebuilt. Here are preserved the relics of Guru Gobind Singh including his cradle, weapons and Proclamations.

The third seat of authority is called "Takhat Sri Kesgarh Sahib" The township of Anandpur was founded by the Ninth Guru in 1665 but the Takhat therein owes its importance to the creation of the Khalsa by Guru Gobind Singh in 1699. The Shrine contains the historic double-edged-sword-*Khanda* with which the Guru stirred the *Amrit* (baptism-water). It has also a number of weapons of the Tenth Guru. During the annual Holi festival, mock-battles between groups of Sikhs are held here. This is called the Hola Mahalla festival by the Sikhs.

The fourth seat of authority is "Takhat Sri Huzur Sahib". It is the place where Guru Gobind Singh passed away in 1708 and is situated at Nander in Maharashtra State. Maharaja Ranjit Singh renovated the temple and provided a gold-plated dome and several costly decorations. The Takhat puts on display the weapons of Guru Gobind Singh and other relics on Sikh festivals. Some manuscript copies of the *Dasam Granth* can be seen here.

The fifth seat of authority is called "Takhat Damdama Sahib". This place owes its importance to the literary work of Guru Gobind Singh done during his stay in 1706. Here the Tenth Guru prepared the authentic edition of the Adi Granth, to which he gave prepetual succession at the time of his death. The Guru held his court at Damdama Sahib for over nine months and imparted training in arts of war and peace to his followers.

The five Takhats have authority in their respective jurisdictions, and recommend punishments for specific religious offences called 'Tankha'. The daily routine of prayers etc. follows an old tradition. Only the best Sikhs are selected as heads (Jathedars) of these five Takhats.

119. **Explain the procedure and significance of Gurmatta (Guru's Decision).**

Gurmatta or Guru's decision is a special resolution passed by the corporate personality of the Sikh community. Its features are as under:

(i) Gurmatta may be taken only by one of the five Takhats in the presence of the Guru Granth Sahib.

(ii) 'The five beloved ones' (Punj Piyara) including the Head (Jathedar) are selected by the participants on basis of merit, piety and religious living.

(iii) The persons present must have no enmity against one another, and must declare their impartiality; personal differences cannot be expressed here.

(iv) The subject must be of concern to the entire Sikh Community, and must not pertain to the interests of a group or party of Sikhs.

(v) The Gurmatta has to be unanimous; there is no question of majority view.

(vi) The Gurmatta is binding on all Sikhs; they must respect and implement it, though they may not be personally in favour of it.

So, in essence, Gurmatta is a "decision of the collective will of the Sikh community" It is the symbol and form of the supreme authority of the *Panth.* It has the sanction of the Guru Granth Sahib and the entire Sikh Community. The solution of new problems facing the community can be sought through the institution of Gurmatta.

One of the important Gurmattas passed in 1747 was the nomination of Sardar Jassa Singh Ahluwalia as the Commander of the Dal Khalsa against the forces of Ahmed Shah Abdali. In December, 1920, Gurmatta was passed for liberating Sikh Gurdwaras from proprietory control, and bringing them under popular administration. Gurmattas are taken in cases of emergency or when a crisis faces the Sikh community as a whole.

120. Give a brief survey of Sikh Studies.

Sikh studies in its broadest sense means creative literature on Sikh History, Sikh Philosophy, culture and fine arts. Such studies may be divided in five headings.

Historical, Theological, Institutional, Cultural and Practical. Historical studies will cover the lives of the Ten Gurus (1469-1708) persecution of the Sikhs in the eighteenth century and the growth of the *missals,* Sikh rule under Maharaja Ranjit Singh and his successors (1800-1849), Punjab under British rule (1849-1947), Post-independence period (1947 uptodate). The recent period will also include the study of the problems of the Sikhs both in India and abroad.

Theological studies pertain to the teachings of the Gurus, the interpretations of the scriptures, and the concepts of God, Creation, Man, Maya, Ethics, The Holy Word, Meditation, Salvation etc. *Institutional studies include Sangat, Pangat, Gurdwara, Khalsa Brotherhood, Takhats, Gurmatta* etc.

Cultural studies will cover the study of the fine arts of the Sikhs, specially their music (both classical and folk), their architecture (specially

Gurdwara architecture and town planning) their paintings (both secular and religious) etc.

Practical Sikhism includes the Sikh way of life, the family, the community, social commitment, worship, ceremonies, Sikh identity and character.

However the above categories should not be considered as watertight compartments; they are like intersecting circles cutting mutual frontiers. For example Practical Sikhism is nothing but leading family-life according to the message of the Gurus.

India

Sikh studies began in right earnest after the Independence in India in 1947. Principal Jodh Singh, Prof. Teja Singh, Prof. Sahib Singh and Dr. Ganda Singh produced worth-while books on Sikh themes. The establishment of the new universities (Guru Nanak Dev University, Amritsar, Punjab University, Chandigarh; Punjabi University, Patiala) initiated serious research in Sikh religion and history. The celebration of centenaries of Guru Gobind Singh (1966), Guru Nanak (1969), Guru Tegh Bahadur (1975), Guru Amardas (1979) and Maharaja Ranjit Singh (1980) gave impetus to the production of valuable research books on the Gurus and Sikh theme.

Among the recent university Scholars are Prof. Harbans Singh, Narain Singh, S.S. Kohli, G.S. Talib, B.S. Anand, J.S. Grewal, Fauja, singh, Mohinder Singh, H.S. Shan, A.C. Chatterjee, H.R. Gupta, C.H. Leohlin, S.S. Bal, P.S. Gill, Pritam Singh, Prakash Singh, Taran Singh, Mc. Leod, W.O. Cole, Juergensmyer, Shackle and others.

The non-university writers of considerable merit are Dr. Gopal Singh, Khushwant singh, K.S. Duggal, S.Trilochan Singh, Raghbir Singh, Daljeet Singh, Jagjit Singh, G.S. Sidhu, Ishwar Singh, P.S. Sambhi, D. Greenlees, Dr. Gurmeet Singh and Dalip Singh.

The credit for pioneering work in the field of Sikh studies, as for example the preparation of the Sikh Encyclopeadia in several volumes, and the translation of Sri Guru Granth Sahib in modern English (with footnotes) goes to the Punjabi University, Patiala. Its department of Religion and Adi Granth Studies also prepares students for the M. Phill and Ph. D. Degrees.

United Kingdom

Sikh studies in U.K. began with the introduction of Sikhism as one of the sections of the paper on "World Religions" at the GCE Level. Both teachers and students needed books suited to the standards of Britain. Dr. Owen Cole deserves credit for preparing some basic books and reference material on Sikh Studies. His book entitled "World Religions: A Handbook for teachers", which he edited for the SHAP working party on World Religions in Education in 1976 prompted many writers to produce books for the school curriculum. As far as I know about twenty books have been published in U.K. by eminent writers like Dr. Cole, P.S. Sambhi, W.H. Mcleod, Terry Thomas, J.R.S. Whitting, John Prickett and others. Perhaps some more books are needed for the GCE. 'A' level.

Sikh studies has found a place in the B.A. course of the Open University, and the first Degree at the West Sussex Institute of Higher Education, Chichester. Leeds and London Universities have provision for research degrees in Sikh Studies. In view of the large number of Sikhs settled in Britian, there is a great need for a centre of Sikh Studies and Research. Perhaps after collection of adequate funds, such a centre can be established either at Sally Oak College, Birmingham, or West Sussex Institute of Higher Education at Chichester. The proposed centre may also provide training facilities for teachers, teaching Sikhism at the GCE level.

Canada

Though the first Sikh immigrants settled on the west coast of Canada in 1905, Sikh Studies has not received its due place either at the school or college level. The Sikhs have been more concerned with ethnic, economic and political issues than their religion or the cultural upbringing of their children. There is a large number of Sikhs in Toronto, Vancouver, and a sizeable number at Calgary, Edmonton and Ottawa. The Sikhs have been holding Annual Conferences since 1979, where issues like identity of the Sikhs, Sikh children and their education, the relations with other communities, Sikhs in small towns and the means of communication with their coreligionists, Sikh women and their role in the new environment are discussed. The number of books on Sikhism published in Canada is very small. Most of them deal with the problems of immigration and employment. The main reason for the neglect of Sikh studies is the indifference of the State and the preoccupation of Sikhs with Gurdwara politics.

Moreover, the Sikhs are mostly working in trade and industry, and very few are in the learned professions. G.S. Pannu's "Sikhs in Canada" is a learned treatise presented to the University of British Columbia (1970) posing the problems facing the Sikh community. Another work dealing with ethnic problems of the Sikhs written by T.J. Scanlon entitled "The Sikhs of Vancouver: a case-study of the Role of the Media in Ethnic relations" was published by UNESCO (Paris) in 1977. Till such time as Sikh Studies is made a subject at the school or college level, no worthwhile publications may be forth-coming in Canada.

United States of America

Though Sikh Studies has not been accepted as a subject at the school level, on account of the separation of the State from Religion in the USA, perhaps a beginning can be made in Sikh Studies in cities where the Sikhs are settled in large numbers. California has a rich and viable group of both Sikh farmers and professional men, and many have expressed the need of a Public school in a place like Yuba City. The Gurdwaras and Sikh Associations have hardly taken any interest in Sikh Studies. There is the Sikh Council of North America but it is suffering from factionalism and petty politics. Individuals have written some books on Sikh themes. Besides Archer's 'The Sikhs' (1946), Dr. S.S. Ahluwalia's book (God's Free Kitchen, 1979) and Khushwant Singh's two Volumes (History of the Sikhs 1966) have been published in the States.

There is however an organised group of America-born Sikhs under the 3HO (also called the Sikh Dharma Brotherhood) managed by the Khalsa Council. Their leader Yogi Harbhajan Singh has promoted Sikhism and published a few books (The experience of consciousness, and The Saying of Yogi Bhajan, 1977). Their publications include "Siblings of Destiny," "Japji of Guru Nanak," "Sikh Dharma Training Manual," "The Sun Shall rise in the West" and some others. Their books include the two notable works published in 1976, by Premka Kaur ("Peace Lagoon: Selections from the Sikh Scriptures": and "Guru for the Aquarian Age: Life of Guru Nanak").

There are two university centres which provide facilities for research in Sikh religion. One is the Department of Religion at the University of California, Berkley, San Francisco. The section of Sikh Studies is under the charge of Dr. Juergensmyer who compiled a number of papers on various aspects of Sikhism under the title "Sikh Studies, Berkley", in 1980. In 1982, Prof. Harbans Singh of Patiala delivered three lectures at Berkley, which were later published under the title "Berkley Lectures", by Guru Nanak Foundation, New Delhi.

The other place is the Centre for the Study of World Religions at Harvard University. The Guru Nanak Foundation of North America, Maryland, the Guru Gobind Singh Foundation, Maryland, The Sikh Philosophical Society, Columbia, the Research and Educational Centre, Chesterfield, St. Louis, may pool their resources in the near future and set up a joint centre for Sikh Studies and Research on the East Coast.

South-East Asia

Sikhs are settled in Malaysia, Indonesia, Singapore and Hong Kong in large numbers. They have built up many Gurdwaras in major cities. Singapore has the distinction of leading the other regions in Sikh Studies. Two books have been written and published by Mehervan Singh on "Sikhism" and "Sikhism in Malaysia". The latter highlights the problems of the local Sikhs. Recently, the Guru Nanak Satsang Sabha, and the Missionary Society of Singapore got approved "Sikh Studies" as subject for the GCE Course. It is a compact course dealing with all the important aspects of Sikh History and religion. Two books "Hand Book of Sikh Studies" for students, and the other entitled, "Manual of Sikh Studies" for teachers, have been printed in Singapore, perhaps such books will set the pace for the preparation of standard text books on Sikhism in other countries.

121. What is the future of Sikhism?

The Sikhs in glorious past have had long periods of persecution and suffering. Their faith in the Gurus and God, and an awareness of the need for voluntary community service made them face cheerfully, many ordeals. The eighteenth century witnessed the genocide of the Sikhs, particularly at the two holocausts of 1746 and 1762 called *Chotta Ghallughara and Wada Ghallughara* respectively, from which the Sikhs rose like phoenix from the ashes. Their martyrdom has, inspired successive generations of Sikhs to the cause of the *Panth* and their belief in *Chardi Kala*, Dynamic optimism.

Again during this century, the Partition of India in 1947 divided their home-land and dealt them another catastrophic blow, physically and economically. Again they never lost the courage and will to survive. Many of them migrated to the truncated Punjab, others went to foreign countries and established themselves. In the new state of the Punjab, they brought in, the *Green Revolution* (in agriculture) and the White Revolution (in milk production). Now Punjab, has the highest per capita income in India. Though affluence has brought in some evils the Sikhs have managed to maintain their vitality and leadership in both the economic and political fields by hard work, sociability, resourcefulness and optimism.

The world of today is torn by strife and suffering. Even the affluent countries are not free from the fear of war and the dilution of their quality of life. Man has progressed materially but not intrinsically. Disparities in income, the poverty of two-thirds of the world's population, the maldistribution of resources and the exploitation of the weaker sections of humanity, have divided the globe into the North and the South—the Industrial nations and the Under-developed nations. The Gurus showed a way forward to the removal of inequity through justice, equality and freedom. Religion in its true sense is not of ritual, but of fellowship and self-discipline. Hypocrisy and double standards erode our character and hinder our progress. A Sikh's recognition of the brotherhood of all ordinary people is illustrated in *Sangat* (congregation) and *Pangat* (Free kitchen). The Gurus' love of humanity made them declare that there was truth in all revelation. Man must follow and practise sincerely, the commands of his own religion.

Today we witness a revival of Sikhism all over the world. Sikhs are discovering the truth of the Gurus' message by studying *Gurbani*. Non-Sikhs are being influenced by the zeal and dedication of Sikhs to projects of community-welfare and voluntary service. More Sikhs are taking *Amrit* as they try to become Guru Gobind Singh's saint-soldiers. The growth of Sikhism in the United States of America is a testimony to the relevance and vitality of the Gurus' teachings in this day and age. Not only there is great increase in the number of Sikhs, but also a new enthusiasm to follow the teachings of the Gurus in daily life. Sikhism is now a World Religion, it has a great part to play in building bridges of understanding and friendship between the different nations of the world and in the promotion of global peace.

Section VII
Sikhism and Modern Problems

122. What is the Sikh attitude to dancing?

Dancing is a mode of entertainment in western countries. Sikhism applies the general test mentioned in the Scripture to any entertainment, namely, "Avoid that which causes pain or harm to the body or produces evil thoughts in the mind." (AG, 16) Dancing with partners of the opposite sex is likely to cause sensuous thoughts, for intimate bodily movements rouse the lower passions.

However, cultural dances like *Bhangra, Gidda, Tiranjan* etc. are not forbidden, but these should not be performed in the presence of Guru Granth Sahib. Such dances are meant for social occasions or festivals and have no religious significance. There are other religious dances which are done by the Hindus (as for example Ras-Lila), and also by Muslim Sufi mystics. Such dances are not permitted in Sikhism. What the Guru permitted was 'the dance of the mind', and not of the body. The Guru says:

"O my mind, dance before the Guru;

If you dance according to the will of the Guru.

You will gain happiness, and the fear of death will vanish." (AG, 506).

This kind of dance is the result of spiritual ecstasy, and is free from physical jerking or gymnastics.

Similar is the Sikh attitude to Discotheque. Disco is a blend of physical movements related to loud pop music. The lights in the hall or the room are deliberately kept dim to enable the partners to get closer and make love easier. As disco is likely to arouse sexual feelings, it is not permitted to the Sikhs. Dances purely for the promotion of physical health or fitness are not taboo. Similarly dating or mixing of boys with girls alone for the purpose of illicit love or petting or flirting is forbidden in Sikhism. However, the meeting of a boy with a girl in the presence of their parents or elders of the community in connection with a marriage proposal is permissible.

123. What is the Sikh attitude to divorce?

Sikhism favour family life and monogamy. The ideal family is one where there is mutual love and respect between the husband and wife and their children and grand children if any. The Anand Marriage Act, 1909, gave a wife status equal to that of her husband. The marriage establishes a permanent relationship between the partners and there is no provision for divorce under this Act, for the Sikh marriage (Anand Karaj) is a sacrament and not a civil contract. However, in olden times if the marriage broke down, the woman would leave her husband and go and stay with her parents. Nowadays, the partners may live separately, or apply for a divorce after some time, under the Hindu Code or the civil marriage Act. At that time, it is for the court to decide to grant a divorce or not, and in case the divorce is decided by the Court, it may make a provision for the support of the woman and the custody of the children and their maintenance. The Sikhs have no Personal Law, but they are covered under the Hindu Code in India. However, in certain cases, the custom of *chaddar*, which implies the present of a bedsheet by a man to a woman indicating his decision to take her as his wife is legal in Punjab.

Generally, grounds like cruelty, adultery, change of religion, suffering from an incurable disease and in some cases incompatibility of temperaments are accepted by Courts for purposes of divorce. A second marriage after divorce is permissible. The remarriage of a widow or widower is encouraged in Sikhism.

124. What is the Sikh attitude to Family-planning?

In olden times, the problem of family-planning did not exist. Even today, in areas where population is scanty and resources adequate, family-planning is not necessary. This does not mean that excessive indulgence in sex becomes desirable. The Gurus told their followers to exercise self-control and to regulate sex sensibly. The Gurus recommended the middle way between self-indulgence and abstinance. Excessive sex was taboo as it led to sorrow and sickness.

Sikhism accepts the common-sense approach to family-planning. It is for the couple to decide whether they want family-planning or not, and in case the answer is in the affirmative, the mode or technique thereof. Family-planning may be necessary for health of the partners or the nursing or up-bringing of existing children. However, natural methods of contraception are preferred to artificial methods and devices. Even so, family-planning should not be under-taken without competent medical advice and supervision. There are no injunctions in Sikhism against the use of contraceptives. Abortion is taboo, as it is an interference in the creative work of God. If the conception has taken place, it would be a sin to destroy life and hence deliberate miscarriage or abortion is forbidden. Similarly, experimenting with embryos and genes is discouraged. Contraception for the purpose of avoiding the results of illicit sex is also forbidden.

125. What is the Sikh attitude to mercy-killing?

Today there is a lot of pressure of politicians to legalise mercy-killing. In certain countries, mercy-killing of patients suffering from incurable diseases or terminal illness has been regulated by law. It is left either to the discretion of the physician or the patient. Recently a new Society named "EXIT" has been started in Great Britain, which supports the right of the individual to die with dignity and its literature contains some instructions for those who desire a painless suicide. The tendency towards the death-wish is fostered by present-day tensions and the conflicts of our competitive society. Mental illness is on the increase, and some people, in a fit of depression, may welcome death as a relief from the torture of living.

What is the Sikh view on this important subject of Euthanasia or mercy-killing? It is right to end a life on account of the pain and agony faced by a patient. Is the physician under a duty to end life, when the terminally ill patient asks for relief in death? The Gurus regarded suffering as a result of man's Karma. Man must have the moral courage to bear his suffering without lament. He should pray for the grace of God to enable him to put up with pain in a spirit of resignation and surrender.

There is no place for mercy-killing in Sikhism. The Gurus tackled the problem of sickness and suffering by providing medical relief and alleviation of pain. Guru Arjan built a leprosarium at Tarn-Taran. Guru Har Rai established a hospital at Kiratpur. It is reported that he supplied a rare herb to emperor Jahangir for the serious illness of his son. After all suffering is a part of the human condition and has a place in God's scheme. Suffering also prompts man to turn his thoughts to God; "Suffering is a medicine; happiness is a disease."

The Gurus rejected suicide, as it is an interference in God's plan.

Many Sikhs faced torture and ultimate death at the hands of tyrant rulers and fanatic leaders, though they could have found relief through suicide. Birth and death are the prerogatives of God and under His command, and it is no business of man to oppose the Divine will.

Recently, the Pope condemned mercy-killing and suicide as opposed to God's will and declared it as a crime of the utmost gravity. It is the duty of the State and society to alleviate the suffering of citizens by medicines, surgery or psychological treatment. Even the expert physician has no right as such to end life. If he cannot cure or heal, he should not destroy life.

Glossary

Amrit	: The Water of immortality; this term is applied to the baptism-ceremony of the Sikhs.
Ardas	: The General Prayer, of the Sikhs, in which a Sikh makes a request to God.
Atma	: The self, the spirit, the soul.
Avtar	: Incarnation, rebirth.
Bhagat	: Saint, holy man.
Brahmgiani	: God-illumined soul, a man who has realised God.
Chitt	: Mind-stuff, heart.
Darshan	: Vision of divine light, a system of philosophy.
Daswand	: One-tenth of income, donated by Sikhs for charitable purposes.
Daya	: Mercy, compassion.
Dharam	: Righteousness, duty, religion.
Dhyan	: Concentration, meditation.
Gunas	: The three Basic attributes.
Grahsta	: The life of a householder.
Gurbani	: The utterance of the Teacher, here hymns in the Guru Granth Sahib—The Guru's words.
Gurmat	: Philosophy of the teachings of the Gurus.
Gurmukh	: One who follows the Guru's teaching.
Gurdwara	: Guru's door, a Sikh temple.
Hukam	: Command, Will of God, a random reading from the Guru Granth Sahib.
Jaikara	: The Sikh cry: Jo bolay so nihal, Sat Sri Akal.
Kam	: Sex, lust.
Karma	: The Law of action and reaction.
Khalsa	: The Pure in heart—an enlightened one.
Khalsa Panth	: The organisation founded by the tenth Guru.
Krodh	: Anger
Kirtan	: Singing of the praises of God.—Hymn singing.
Lavan	: Marriage hymns.
Lobh	: Greed, avarice.
Manmukh	: Self-willed, irreligious person—the opposite to Gurmukh.

Massands	: Professional priests.
Maya	: Worldiness, illusion.
Missal	: A Community or confederacy.
Moh	: Attachment.
Mukti (Moksha)	: Liberation, salvation.
Nam	: Divine Name, the Holy spirit, the spirit of God.
Panth	: Path of life, the community of Sikhs.
Parchar	: Missionary work.
Raga	: An Indian musical pattern or score.
Raj yoga	: Spiritual Union in worldly glory.
Sadhana	: Spiritual effort, right action.
Samadhi	: State of contemplation, merger with the Infinite.
Sahaj yoga	: The Natural serenity obtained in spiritual union or perfection.
Sanyasa	: Asceticism, renunciation of the world.
Satsang	: Holy company, prayer meeting, a devotional group in action.
Shabad	: A hymn of praise to God.
Shakti	: Cosmic energy, nature, God's power
Sidh	: Hermit, Yogi of Gorakh cult.
Sidhis	: Occult powers.
Simran	: Meditation, constant remembrance of God —Practising the presence of God.
Turya	: The fourth stage, highest spiritual state.
Vairag	: Distaste for worldly things.
Vedas	: Sacred scriptures of the Hindus.
Waheguru	: "Wonderful Lord", the Sikh Mantra.
Wismad	: Feeling of wonder, ecstasy.
Yoga	: Union with God, occult practices.

Select Bibliography

Cole & Sambhi   : The Sikhs, London 1978.

Field Dorothy   : Religion of the Sikhs, London, 1914.

Gopal Singh   : A History of the Sikh People (1469-1978) Delhi, 1979.

Greenlees D   : The Gospel of the Granth Sahib, Madras, 1968.

Gupta H.R.   : History of the Sikh Gurus, Delhi, 1973.

Harbans Singh   : The Heritage of the Sikhs, Asia, London 1964.

Jodh Singh   : Some Studies in Sikhism, Ludhiana 1953.

Johar S.S.   : Handbook on Sikhism, Delhi, 1977.

Khushwant Singh   : History of the Sikhs, 2 Vols. 1966.

Kohli S.S.   : Outlines of Sikh Thought, Delhi 1977.

Macauliffe   : The Sikh Religion, 6 Vols; 1909.

Mansukhani G.S.   : Quintessence of Sikhism, Amritsar, 1965.

Mansukhani G.S.   : Aspects of Sikhism 1982.

McLeod   : Guru Nanak and Sikh Religion 1968.

Punjabi University,   : Sikhism, 1969.
Patiala

Sher Singh   : Philosophy of Sikhism, Delhi, 1966.

Teja Singh   : Sikhism—Its ideals and institutions, Amritsar, 1970.

Teja Singh &   : A short history of the Sikhs, Bombay, 1950.
Ganda Singh

INDEX